Collins

KS2 Revision
Maths

Maths

Age 7 – 11

Key Stage 2

Revision Guide

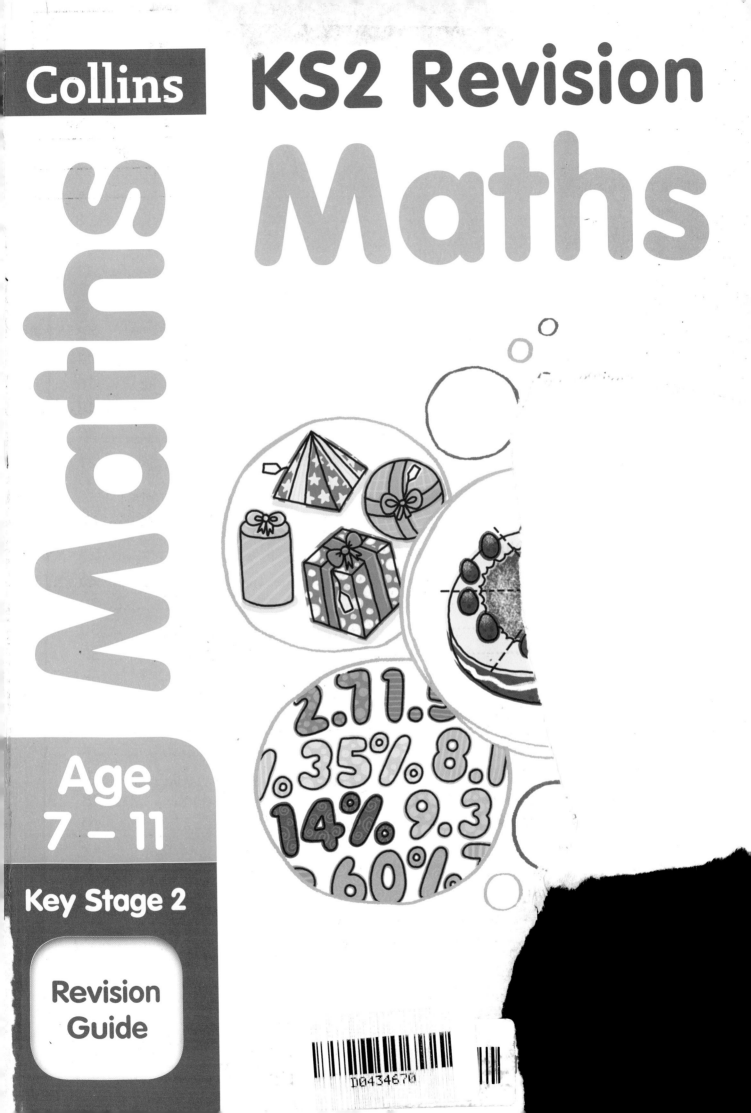

Contents

Ordering Numbers

You need to look at numbers to compare them and find out which number is greater.

Example

Which is greater? 3715 or 3742 ✓

Both numbers have 3 thousands and 7 hundreds so we need to look at the next column – the **tens** column – to compare them.

3715 ← has 1 TEN

3742 ← has 4 TENS

This means 3742 is greater than 3715.

You can write 'greater than' and 'less than' using symbols:
> means 'is **greater than**'
< means 'is **less than**'

So 3742 > 3715

Quick Test

1. Write these numbers in figures: a) 32 946 b) 5499
   a) Thirty-two thousand nine hundred and forty-six
   b) Three hundred and fifty-four thousand six hundred and ninety-three
2. What value does the number 5 have in each of these numbers? Tens, hundreds or ten thousands may be preferred as answers.
   a) 456   b) 52 341   c) 6513
3. Put these numbers in order from largest to smallest:
   4315   4324   4253   4135   4335
4. Put > or < between these pairs of numbers to make the statements correct:
   a) 2315 < 4643   b) 5419 > 5416
   c) 32 556 > 32 546   d) 101 322 > 10 132

5

Negative Numbers

- Understand negative numbers
- Count forwards and backwards with positive and negative numbers
- Find the next terms in a sequence

What are Negative Numbers?

Numbers below zero are called **negative numbers**. They have a 'minus' sign in front of them to show that they are negative numbers, for example –14, –465.

If you look at a number line, you can see that negative numbers count from 0 in the opposite direction to **positive numbers**.

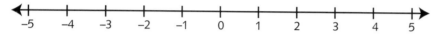

Key Point

We know that positive numbers get greater (bigger) as we count in this direction.
In the same way, negative numbers also get greater as you count in this direction. ⟶

Example

5 is greater than 2.

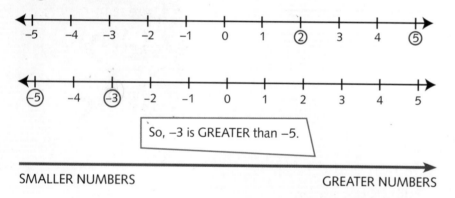

So, –3 is GREATER than –5.

SMALLER NUMBERS   GREATER NUMBERS

Key Point

The nearer a negative number is to zero on a number line, the greater or bigger it is.

Counting Using Negative Numbers

You can count back from 10 in 2s by taking away 2 each time:

If you continue to count back in 2s, you can go beyond zero into negative numbers.

Counting Sequences

You can count on or back from any number in equal steps. This is called a **sequence**.

You need to be able to count on or back from any number in jumps of any size.

Example

Counting from 5 in steps of 4:   5, 9, 13, 17…

Count back in 100s from 953:   953, 853, 753…

Sometimes you are not given the steps.

Example

What are the next three **terms** or numbers in this sequence?

4, 10, 16, _____ _____ _____

First you need to work out the jump between each number in our sequence.

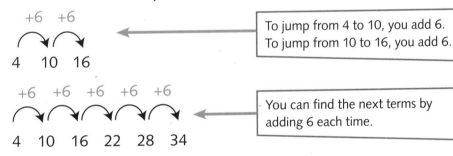

To jump from 4 to 10, you add 6.
To jump from 10 to 16, you add 6.

You can find the next terms by adding 6 each time.

Quick Test

1. Order these numbers from smallest to largest:
   10 –3 5 –9 6 –2 0 –5
2. Fill in the next three terms counting back in 3s:
   4 1 –2 _–5_ _–8_ _–11_
3. Fill in the next three terms counting on in 50s:
   –50 0 _50_ _100_ _150_

Rounding

- Round numbers to the nearest 10, 100, 1000
- Round numbers to the nearest 10 000 or 100 000

Rounding Numbers

Rounding numbers makes them easier to work with and can help you to estimate answers to calculations.

> **Key Point**
>
> When you round numbers, you are asked to round them **'to the nearest...'** 10, 100, 1000, etc.

Example

To round **32** to the nearest **10**, you have a choice of rounding to 30 or 40:

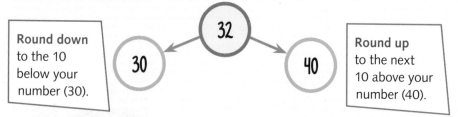

Round down to the 10 below your number (30).

Round up to the next 10 above your number (40).

When you look at a number line, you can see that 32 is nearer to 30 than 40. So you round 32 down to 30.

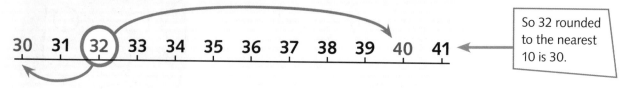

So 32 rounded to the nearest 10 is 30.

The key for rounding to the nearest 10 is the **units**. If the units are less than 5, you **round down**. If the units are 5 or above, you **round up**.

> **Tip**
>
> You could sketch a number line to help you. On a number line you would see that 365 is nearer 400 than 300.

Example

Round 365 to the nearest 100.

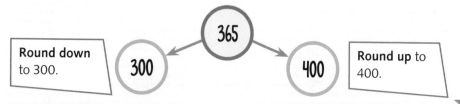

Round down to 300.

Round up to 400.

The key for rounding to the nearest 100 is the **tens** column. If the tens digit is less than 5, **round down**. If the tens digit is 5 or above, **round up**.

The tens digit in 365 is a 6, so you round up to 400. So 365 rounded to the nearest 100 is 400.

To round to the nearest 1000, you need to look at the **hundreds** column. If the hundreds digit is 5 or above, **round up**. If the hundreds digit is below 5, **round down**.

Example

Round 4765 to the nearest 1000.

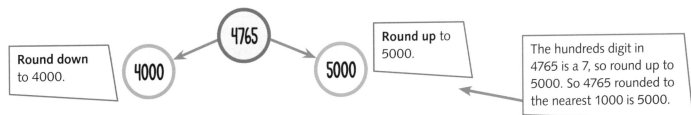

Round down to 4000.

4000

4765

5000

Round up to 5000.

The hundreds digit in 4765 is a 7, so round up to 5000. So 4765 rounded to the nearest 1000 is 5000.

Rounding to the Nearest 10 000 or 100 000

To round to the nearest 10 000, look at the **thousands** digit. If it is 5 or above, **round up**. If it is below 5, **round down**.

Example

2**3** 725 to the nearest 10 000 would round down to 20 000 because the thousands digit is a 3.

To round to the nearest 100 000, you look at the **tens of thousands** digit. If it is 5 or above, **round up**. If it is below 5, **round down**.

Example

5**8**3 725 to the nearest 100 000 would round up to 600 000 because the tens of thousands digit is an 8.

Quick Test

1. Round 64 318 to the nearest:
   a) 10   **b)** 100   **c)** 1000   **d)** 100 000

Key Words

- Round down
- Round up

Roman Numerals

- Read and recognise Roman numerals

Roman Numerals

The Romans used some of the letters from the **Latin alphabet** (I, V, X, L, C, D and M) to represent numbers:

Letter	I	V	X	L	C	D	M
Value	1	5	10	50	100	500	1000

Example

- 5 = V, so 4 = IV (one less than 5) and 6 = VI (one more than 5)
- 10 = X, so 9 = IX (one less than 10) and 11 = XI (one more than 10)
- X can be placed before L to make 40 (XL) and before C to make 90 (XC).
- C can be placed before D to make 400 (CD) and before M to make 900 (CM).

Recording Years in Roman Numerals

The Romans were one of the first civilisations to use calendars, so they recorded the years using their number system.

Example

2015 would be recorded as MMXV:

1000	1000	10	5
M	M	X	V

> **Key Point**
>
> By placing letters before or after other letters, the Roman system could make any number.

1	I		11	XI
2	II		12	XII
3	III		13	XIII
4	IV		14	XIV
5	V		15	XV
6	VI		16	XVI
7	VII		17	XVII
8	VIII		18	XVIII
9	IX		19	XIX
10	X		20	XX

> **Key Point**
>
> The Romans did not have a **symbol** for zero – they just left it out!

Quick Test

1. Write these Roman numerals as numbers:
   a) XXIII *23*   b) XLVI *66*   c) CCXCIII *393*
2. What years do these Roman numerals represent?
   a) MDCLXVI *1666*   b) MLXVI *1066*   c) MCMXIV *2116*

> **Key Words**
>
> - Latin alphabet
> - Symbol

Practice Questions

Challenge 1

1 Write this number in figures:

forty-six thousand two hundred and twenty-eight _____

1 mark

2 Order these numbers from smallest to largest:

701   107   170   710   1071   _____

1 mark

3 Counting back in 5s, what are the next three terms in this sequence?

14   9   4   _____   _____   _____

3 marks

4 Round 3426 to the nearest:

a) 10 _____   b) 100 _____

2 marks

Challenge 2

1 Which number is closest to 500?

548   515   489   5050   450   _____

1 mark

PS 2 Here are three digit cards. Write **all** the **three-digit** numbers
greater than 600 that can be made using these cards:

5   6   8

_____   _____   _____   _____

4 marks

3 What year do these numerals represent? MCMXLV _____

1 mark

Challenge 3

1 What are the next three terms of this sequence?

17   25½   34   _____   _____   _____

3 marks

2 Anne Boleyn was executed in 1536.
Write this date in Roman numerals.   _____

1 mark

PS 3 Look at this sequence: 7   12   17 ...

Does 96 appear in this sequence? How do you know?

_____

1 mark

4 Round 345 637 to the nearest:

a) 10 _____   b) 100 _____

c) 10 000 _____   d) 100 000 _____

4 marks

11

Number Facts for Mental Calculations

- Know number bonds to 100
- Learn tricks for adding and subtracting

Number Bonds

You need to revise your **number bonds** to 10, 20 and even 100, so that you can find out the missing bond.

Example

$32 + ? = 100$

To help find the other half of the bond, look at the **units** first.

$2 + ? = 10$ $2 + \mathbf{8} = 10$ ← What number bond to 10 goes with 2?

$32 + \mathbf{8} = 40$ ← Add that on to the number.

Now let's look at the **tens**.

$40 + ? = 100$ $40 + \mathbf{60} = 100$ ← What number bond to 100 goes with 40?

So you now know that $32 + \mathbf{8} + \mathbf{60} = 100$

$32 + \mathbf{68} = 100$

Tricks for Adding and Subtracting

Sometimes you can use tricks to make your calculations easier. This is called calculating and **adjusting**.

Example 1

$23 + 9$

If you think of the 9 as a 10 ($9 + 1$), it's easier to add:

$23 + 10 = 33$

But remember you added 10 instead of 9, so you must **subtract** 1 from the answer:

$33 - 1 = 32$

$23 + 9 = 32$

Tip

Make your adjustment at the end of your calculation.

12

Example 2

23 + 11

In the same way, you can think of 11 as a 10 (11 − 1):

23 + 10 = 33

But remember you added 10 instead of 11, so you must **add** 1 more to the answer:

33 + 1 = 34   23 + 11 = 34

This trick works for subtraction too!

Example

42 − 9

Think of the 9 as a 10:

42 − 10 = 32

But remember you took away 10 instead of 9, so you must **add** 1 to the answer:

32 + 1 = 33   42 − 9 = 33

You can use this trick to add bigger numbers.

Example

50 + 199

Add 1 to make 199 into 200 (199 + 1).

Calculate: 50 + 200 = 250

Then adjust: 250 − 1 = 249

50 + 199 = 249

Key Point

Always check that you have adjusted correctly; do you need to add or subtract?

Quick Test

1. Find the missing numbers: a) 66   b 18   c) 35
   a) 26 + ? = 100   b) 78 + ? = 100   c) 465 + ? = 500
2. Use tricks of adding and subtracting to work out these calculations: a) 57   b) 38   c) 447 d) 266
   a) 68 + 11   b) 47 − 9   c) 397 + 50   d) 296 − 30

Key Words

• Number bonds
• Adjust

More Mental Addition and Subtraction

- Add and subtract multiples of 10
- Estimate by rounding
- Add and subtract numbers mentally

Adding and Subtracting Multiples of 10

You can simplify addition calculations involving **multiples of 10**.

Example

$70 + 150$ ← Divide both sides by 10.

$7 + 15$

You can easily calculate $7 + 15 = 22$

So $70 + 150 = 220$ ← Put the 0 back on to each side.

This method of simplifying works for subtraction too!

$140 - 90$

$14 - 9 = 5$

So $140 - 90 = 50$

Estimating Answers

It helps to **estimate** what the answer might be before you start calculating. Then you can check your answer against your estimate to see if it's correct. You estimate by **rounding** the numbers.

Key Point

Round numbers up or down to find an estimate.

Example

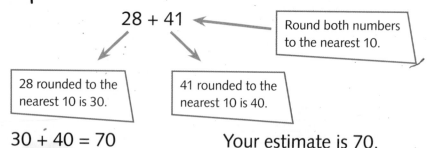

$28 + 41$ ← Round both numbers to the nearest 10.

28 rounded to the nearest 10 is 30.

41 rounded to the nearest 10 is 40.

$30 + 40 = 70$ Your estimate is 70.

Then calculate mentally: $20 + 8 + 40 + 1 = 69$ and check it against the estimate.
The answer is close to the estimate, so you know you must be correct!

Mental Addition

To add numbers mentally (in your head), it can help to partition them into **hundreds**, **tens** and **units**.

Example

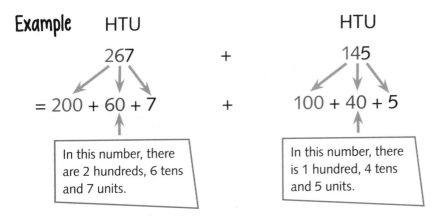

HTU

267   +

= 200 + 60 + 7   +

In this number, there are 2 hundreds, 6 tens and 7 units.

HTU

145

100 + 40 + 5

In this number, there is 1 hundred, 4 tens and 5 units.

You can put the numbers into an order which makes them easier to add up:

200 + 100 + 60 + 40 + 7 + 5

300   + 100   + 12   = 412

Mental Subtraction

You can use partitioning to subtract numbers too.

Example

68 – 43

= 60 + 8 – 40 – 3   ←   Partition each side into tens and units.

= 60 – 40 + 8 – 3

= 20 + 5 = 25

68 – 43 = 25

Quick Test

Use your mental maths skills to work out these. Estimate your answers first.
1. Henry had 18 pens and his sister Ava had 23. How many pens did they have altogether? 41
2. a) 69 + 99 168 b) 302 – 50 248 c) 198 + 45 243

Written Addition

- Add numbers by writing them down
- Add decimals

Addition Using the Column Method

If you are given a sum and the numbers are too big or there are too many numbers to add mentally, then you can use a written method.

You can use the **column method** to add numbers.

Example 1

Jo has collected 243 football cards and Zara has collected 142 cards. How many cards do the children have altogether?

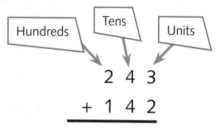

Hundreds   Tens   Units

```
   2  4  3
+  1  4  2
```

1. Start with the **least significant digit** so add the units first.

```
   2  4  3
+  1  4  2
         5
```

2. Then add the tens.

```
   2  4  3
+  1  4  2
      8  5
```

3. Finally, add the hundreds.

```
   2  4  3
+  1  4  2
   3  8  5
```

Key Point

Always make sure your digits are in line with each other in the correct column.

Example 2

Ahmed has 346 stamps in his collection. His friend Sam has 267 stamps in his collection. How many stamps do the boys have in total?

Add the units: 6 + 7 = 13

```
  3  4  6
+ 2  6₁ 7
        3
```

Record the 3 in the units column and **carry** the 10 as a 1 in the tens column:

Then add the tens: 4 + 6 + 1 = 11

```
  3  4  6
+ 2₁ 6₁ 7
     1  3
```

Record the 11 as 1 in the tens column and carry the 10 as a 1 into the hundreds column.

Finally, add the hundreds: 3 + 2 + 1 = 6

```
  3  4  6
+ 2₁ 6₁ 7
  6  1  3
```

Key Point

Sums like this one are more tricky as you have to carry a number to another column. Make sure you carry the number to the next column.

Adding Decimals

Some numbers contain a **decimal point**, for example 13.51 You can use the column method to add decimals.

Example

Saira has saved £34.62 in pocket money. Her auntie gives her another £23.65. How much money does Saira have now?

1. First bring the decimal point down and put it in the answer line directly below the decimal points that are already there.

```
  £ 3 4.6 2
+ £ 2 3.6 5
         .
```

2. Then add the digits using the column method.

```
  £ 3 4 .6 2
+ £ 2 3₁.6 5
  £ 5 8 .2 7
```

Tip

Don't worry about the decimal point: it's already in your answer!

Quick Test

1. Work out these addition calculations by writing them down: **a)** 345 + 62 **b)** 98 + 1090
2. Asif has £32.50 in his money box. Chloe has £14.55. How much money do Asif and Chloe have altogether?

Key Word

• Column method
• Least significant digit
• Carry
• Decimal point

Written Subtraction

- Subtract numbers by writing them down
- Subtract decimals

Subtraction Using the Column Method

You can subtract bigger numbers using the column method. You need to make sure that the digits are all written in the correct column.

Sometimes it helps to put the **place value** labels above your calculation.

Start with the least significant digit (in this calculation – the units).

$4865 - 1342 = ?$

Example

1. Subtract the units: $5 - 2 = 3$

```
  4 8 6 5
- 1 3 4 2
        3
```

2. Then subtract the tens: $6 - 4 = 2$

```
  4 8 6 5
- 1 3 4 2
      2 3
```

3. Then subtract the hundreds: $8 - 3 = 5$

```
  4 8 6 5
- 1 3 4 2
    5 2 3
```

4. Then, finally, the thousands: $4 - 1 = 3$

```
  4 8 6 5
- 1 3 4 2
  3 5 2 3
```

Some calculations can be more tricky:

Example

1. When you look at the units you can't subtract 6 from 3, so you go to the tens column and **exchange** the 7 for a 6 and a 1.

```
  5 2 7 3
- 1 3 4 6
```

2. Now you have $13 - 6$ which you can subtract.

```
      6 1
  5 2 7̸ 3
- 1 3 4 6
        7
```

Tip

It might be helpful to label each column in your calculation with its place value.

3. You then subtract 6 – 4 in the tens column.

```
    6 1
5 2 7̸ 3
- 1 3 4 6
_____
      2 7
```

5273 – 1346 = ?

4. When you look at the hundreds column, you can't subtract 3 from 2 so you go to the thousands column and exchange the 5 for a 4 and a 1. This means you can subtract 12 – 3 = 9.

```
4 1 6 1
5̸ 2 7̸ 3
- 1 3 4 6
_____
    9 2 7
```

5. Then you can finish by subtracting 4 – 1 in the thousands column.

```
4 1 6 1
5̸ 2 7̸ 3
- 1 3 4 6
_____
  3 9 2 7
```

Subtracting Decimals

You can subtract decimals using the same method you used for adding decimals.

Example

You can't subtract 7 from 3 so you need to exchange.

```
  4 7.3
- 2 4.7
```

```
   6 1
4 7̸.3
- 2 4.7
_____
  2 2.6
```

Tip

Remember to drop the decimal point into your answer before you start.

Quick Test

1. Try these calculations. Remember to estimate your answer first.
  a) 3782 – 3131 651
  b) 4126 – 3452 674
  c) 16.83 – 12.96 387

17 – 13

Key Words

- Place value
- Exchange

Practice Questions

Challenge 1

1　Find the number bonds to 100 for these numbers:

　　a) 45 _55_　　　　　　　　　　b) 76 _24_

　　c) 17 _83_　　　　　　　　　　d) 63 _37_

4 marks

2　Work out 70 + 40 mentally. _____

1 mark

3　Work these out using a written method.

　　a)　3417 + 4752　　　　　　　　b) 3415 – 1263

2 marks

Challenge 2

1　Find the number bonds to 1000 for these numbers:

　　a) 465 _____　　　　　　　　　b) 736 _____

　　c) 257 _____　　　　　　　　　d) 666 _____

4 marks

2　Work out 302 – 40 mentally. _____

1 mark

3　Work these out using a written method.

　　a) 7184 – 3276　　　　　　　　b) 24.72 + 15.16

2 marks

Challenge 3

1　49 + 162

　　Using rounding, which estimate is closest? Tick the correct answer.

　　200 ☐　　　　　220 ☐　　　　　210 ☑

1 mark

2　Work out 597 + 301 mentally. _____

1 mark

3　Work these out using a written method.

　　a) £34.67 + £26.99　£61.66　　　b) 16.85 – 11.47

2 marks

Review Questions

1   What value does the digit 5 have in these numbers?

a) 3567 _____

b) 315 _____

c) 543.2 _____

3 marks

2   Put these numbers in order from the smallest to the largest:

314   413   441   341   334

_314   334   341   413   441_____

1 mark

3   Counting back in 100s, what are the next three terms?

515 __415_____ __315_____ __215_____

3 marks

4   Round these numbers to the nearest 10:

a) 64 __60_____   b) 302 __300_____   c) 1278 __1280_____

3 marks

5   Round these numbers to the nearest 100:

a) 365 _____   b) 1193 _____   c) 202 __200_____

3 marks

6   Write the next three numbers in the sequence:

17   21.5   26 __31.5_____ __36_____ __41.5_____

3 marks

7   Write the next three numbers in the sequence:

7   1   –5 __-11_____ __-17_____ _____

3 marks

8   Round these numbers to the nearest 10 000:

a) 46 893 __50 000_____   b) 23 267 __20 000_____   c) 146 623 __150 000_____

3 marks

9   Which is nearer to 500: 478 or 518? Give a reason for your answer.

_518   because   it   is   more   near_____

1 mark

10   Look at the sequence:

14, 20, 26 ....

Is 53 in this sequence? Give a reason for your answer.

_No   because   we   are   adding   6   but   if_____
I   do   the   answer   something   else.

1 mark

11   Write 27 in Roman numerals. __XXVII_____

1 mark

12   What years do these Roman numerals represent?

a) MCMXXXVI _____   b) MMXVIII __2018_____

2 marks

All Kinds of Numbers

- Know the times tables and related division facts
- Learn about factors, multiples and products

Times Tables and Division Facts

You need to know all of the times tables up to 12 × 12:

×	1	2	3	4	5	6	7	8	9	10	11	12
1	1	2	3	4	5	6	7	8	9	10	11	12
2	2	4	6	8	10	12	14	16	18	20	22	24
3	3	6	9	12	15	18	21	24	27	30	33	36
4	4	8	12	16	20	24	28	32	36	40	44	48
5	5	10	15	20	25	30	35	40	45	50	55	60
6	6	12	18	24	30	36	42	48	54	60	66	72
7	7	14	21	28	35	42	49	56	63	70	77	84
8	8	16	24	32	40	48	56	64	72	80	88	96
9	9	18	27	36	45	54	63	72	81	90	99	108
10	10	20	30	40	50	60	70	80	90	100	110	120
11	11	22	33	44	55	66	77	88	99	110	121	132
12	12	24	36	48	60	72	84	96	108	120	132	144

Tip

If you learn these times tables, you will find it easier and quicker to do calculations.

You can use your times table knowledge to find division facts.

Example

$9 \times 8 = 72$ and $8 \times 9 = 72$, so:

$72 \div 8 = 9$ and $72 \div 9 = 8$

Factors, Products and Multiples

Factors are numbers that can be multiplied together to give another number.

Example

3 and 10 are factors of 30 ($3 \times 10 = 30$)

6 and 4 are factors of 24 ($6 \times 4 = 24$)

Products are the answers given by multiplying factors.

Example

6 is the product of 2 × 3 ← 2 and 3 are factors

50 is the product of 5 × 10 ← 5 and 10 are factors

Multiples are the answers you get when you multiply a given number by any other number.

Key Point

Multiples are the answers to our times tables.

Example

Multiples of 5 are: 5, 10, 15, 20, 25…

Common Factors and Common Multiples

Common factors are factors that are common to more than one product.

Example

Factors of 12 are: **1**, **2**, 3, **4**, 6, and 12

Factors of 8 are: **1**, **2**, **4** and 8

So the common factors of 12 and 8 are: 1, 2 and 4.

Common multiples are multiples that are common to two or more numbers.

Example

The multiples of 3 are: 3, **6**, 9, **12**, 15, **18**…

The multiples of 2 are: 2, 4, **6**, 8, 10, **12**, 14, 16, **18**…

So common multiples of 2 and 3 include: 6, 12 and 18.

Quick Test

1. Write the two division facts that are related to 8 × 11 = 88   88 ÷ 11 = 8   88 ÷ 8 = 11
2. List all the factors of 30.   3x10   10x3
3. What is the product of 2, 3 and 4?   24
4. List the common factors of 16 and 20.   4x4   2x10   3x5   10÷2

Key Words

- Factor
- Product
- Multiple
- Common factor
- Common multiple

Prime, Square and Cube Numbers

- Recognise prime numbers
- Recognise prime factors
- Understand square numbers
- Understand cube numbers

Prime Numbers

A **prime number** is a number than can **only** be divided by 1 **and** itself (it only has two factors).

- 1 is **not** a prime number because it can only be divided by 1 (it only has one factor).
- 2 is the only even prime number (because all other even numbers can be divided by 2).
- Other prime numbers are 3, 5, 7, 11, 17…

Key Point

2 is the only even prime number.

Prime Factors

A **prime factor** is a factor that is also a prime number.

3 and 5 are the prime factors of 15 because both 3 and 5 are prime numbers.

Example

To find the prime factors of 36, you first need to look at the factors of 36:

3 and 12 are factors of 36. ($3 \times 12 = 36$)

3 is a prime number but 12 is not, so you need to break 12 down into its factors:

3 and 4 are factors of 12, so now you have:

3, 3 and 4.

4 is not a prime number so again you need to break 4 down into its factors:

2 and 2 are factors of 4. So now you have:

$3 \times 3 \times 2 \times 2 = 36$

So 3, 3, 2 and 2 are the prime factors of 36.

Square Numbers

A **square number** is the answer you get when you multiply any number by itself. The symbol used to show that a number is squared is ^{2} (so, 4^2 means 4 squared).

Example

$4 \times 4 = 4$ squared $= 4^2 = 16$ $\longleftarrow$ 16 is a square number.

$5 \times 5 = 5$ squared $= 5^2 = 25$ $\longleftarrow$ 25 is a square number.

Key Point

The little '2' means squared and the little '3' means cubed.

Cube Numbers

A **cube number** is the answer you get when you multiply any number by itself and by itself again. The symbol used to show that a number is cubed is ^{3} (so, 5^3 means 5 cubed).

Example

$2 \times 2 \times 2 = 2$ cubed $= 2^3 = 8$ $\longleftarrow$ 8 is a cube number.

$3 \times 3 \times 3 = 3$ cubed $= 3^3 = 27$ $\longleftarrow$ 27 is a cube number.

Key Point

Indices or orders include square or cube numbers and square roots.

Order of Operations

Calculations should be carried out using this order of operations:

Brackets, Indices or **Orders, Division, Multiplication, Addition, Subtraction**

Example

$(3 + 6) \times 2^2 + 21 \div (8 - 5) - 5 = 9 \times 2^2 + 21 \div 3 - 5$ $\longleftarrow$ Work out the brackets first.

$= 9 \times 4 + 21 \div 3 - 5$ $\longleftarrow$ Work out the square number next.

$= 36 + 7 - 5 = 38$ $\longleftarrow$ Multiply and divide (from left to right), then add and subtract (from left to right).

Quick Test

1. What is 3 squared? 9
2. What is 4 cubed? 12
3. Find the prime factors of 14. 2 and 7
4. Find a prime number greater than 20 but less than 30.
23 and 29

Key Words

- Prime number
- Prime factor
- Square number
- Cube number

Multiplying and Dividing

- Multiply and divide by 10, 100 and 1000
- Carry out mental multiplication
- Multiply and divide by 0 or 1

Multiplying and Dividing by 10, 100 and 1000

When you multiply or divide by 10, the digits don't change; they just change position.

Example

462.35 × 10

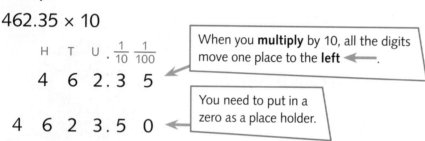

H	T	U	.	$\frac{1}{10}$	$\frac{1}{100}$
4	6	2	. 3	5	

> When you **multiply** by 10, all the digits move one place to the **left** ⟵.

| 4 | 6 | 2 | 3 | . 5 | 0 |

> You need to put in a zero as a place holder.

Because you are multiplying, the answer is bigger than the starting number.

- Each time you multiply by 10, the digits will move **one** place to the left.
- If you multiply by 100 (10 × 10), the digits will move **two** places to the left.
- If you multiply by 1000 (10 × 10 × 10), the digits will move **three** places to the left.

Example

376.2 ÷ 10

H	T	U	.	$\frac{1}{10}$	$\frac{1}{100}$
3	7	6	. 2		

> When you **divide** by 10, the digits move one place to the **right** ⟶.

| 3 | 7 | . 6 | 2 |

Because you are dividing, the answer is smaller than the starting number.

- Each time you divide by 10, the digits will move **one** place to the right.

Tip

Count the zeros in the number you are multiplying or dividing by, then move your digits that many places either to the left (×) or the right (÷).

- If you divide by 100 (10 × 10), the digits will move **two** places to the right.
- If you divide by 1000 (10 × 10 × 10), the digits will move **three** places to the right.

Mental Multiplication

You can **decompose** numbers to help multiply them.

Example

How can you solve 8 × 15?

8 × 15 = 8 × 5 × 3 because 5 × 3 = 15

       = 40 × 3

       = 120

You can also rearrange numbers to make them easier to multiply.

Example

Solve 6 × 8 × 5

= 6 × 5 × 8

= 30 × 8

= 240

6 × 8 × 5 = ?

Multiplying and Dividing by 0 and 1

If you multiply or divide any number by 0, the answer is always 0.

If you multiply or divide any number by 1, the answer is always the number itself.

Quick Test

1. 34.62 × 1000
2. 1753 ÷ 100
3. 8 × 25

Key Point

Remember, multiplication can be done in any order: 3 × 2 = 6 and 2 × 3 = 6

Tip

To multiply by 20, multiply by 10, then double the answer.

To multiply by 5, multiply by 10, then halve the answer.

To divide by 20, divide by 10, then halve the answer.

To divide by 5, divide by 10, then double the answer.

Key Word

- Decompose

Written Multiplication

- Multiply using grids
- Use long multiplication

Grid Multiplication

You can use a grid to work out a multiplication sum.

Example

How can you calculate 24 × 37?

1. Partition each number and write it on a grid.

2. Calculate each answer and write it in the correct space on the grid:

Partition 37 into tens and units. →

×	20	4
30	600	120
7	140	28

← Partition 24 into tens and units.

3. Add up all the answers to get a total:

600 + 120 + 140 + 28 = 888

So, 24 × 37 = 888

Tip

An easy way to multiply 20 × 30 is to think of it as 2 × 10 × 3 × 10 and then rearrange it to make it easier:
2 × 3 × 10 × 10 = 600

Sometimes there might be three or more digits to multiply.

Example

How can you calculate 234 × 5?

1. Treat this the same way: partition each number and write it on the grid.

×	200	30	4
5	1000	150	20

← Partition 234 into hundreds, tens and units.

2. Add up the answers to get a total:

1000 + 150 + 20 = 1170

So, 234 × 5 = 1170

Tip

200 × 5
= 2 × 10 × 10 × 5
= 2 × 5 × 10 × 10
= 1000

Long Multiplication

Another method for working out multiplication by writing it down is called long multiplication.

Example

How can you calculate 38 × 26?

1. Start by multiplying the units by the units:

   6 × 8 = 48. Record the 8 and **carry** the 4 into the next column.

$$\begin{array}{r} 3\ 8 \\ \times\ 2_4\ 6 \\ \hline 8 \end{array}$$

2. Then, multiply the tens by the units:

   6 × 3 = 18 + 4 (that was carried) = 22

$$\begin{array}{r} 3\ 8 \\ \times\ 2_4\ 6 \\ \hline 2\ 2\ 8 \end{array}$$

3. Put a zero in the row below as a place holder.

   Multiply the tens by the units:

   2 × 8 = 16. Record the 6 and carry the 1 into the next column. Last, multiply the tens by the tens:

   2 × 3 = 6 + 1 (that was carried) = 7

$$\begin{array}{r} 3\ 8 \\ \times\ _1 2_4\ 6 \\ \hline 2\ 2\ 8 \\ 7\ 6\ 0 \end{array}$$

4. You then use column addition to find the total:

   228 + 760 = 988

   So, 38 × 26 = 988

$$\begin{array}{r} 3\ 8 \\ \times\ _1 2_4\ 6 \\ \hline 2\ 2\ 8 \\ 7\ 6\ 0 \\ \hline 9\ 8\ 8 \end{array}$$

Tip

It can help you to put a zero in as a place holder. This will prevent you getting digits in the wrong columns.

38 × 26

Quick Test

Work out these calculations using grid multiplication or long multiplication:
1. 5 × 132
2. 28 × 45
3. 1324 × 25
4. 629 × 3

Key Word

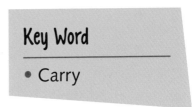

• Carry

Short and Long Division

- Divide by single-digit numbers
- Divide by double-digit numbers

Dividing by Single-Digit Numbers

Short division is sometimes called the 'bus stop' method. You normally use this when you have a single-digit **divisor**.

Example

Calculate 78 ÷ 5

1. Divide the **most significant digit** (in this case the tens digit).
   7 divided by 5 = 1r2.

   Record the 1 above the line and carry the 2 to the next column.

$$5\overline{)7\ \ ^28}$$
$$\phantom{5\overline{)}}1$$

2. Divide 28 (the 2 that was carried has become a ten) by 5 = 5r3.

   Record the 5 above the line and leave a **remainder** of 3.

$$5\overline{)7\ \ ^28}$$
$$\phantom{5\overline{)}}1\ \ \ 5\,r3$$

3. 78 ÷ 5 = 15r3.

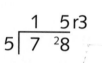

Key Point

The remainder is the amount left over when the number has been divided.

You can express the remainder as:

- a remainder
- a fraction
- a decimal

So, in the example above, the answer would be:

- 15r3 ← As a remainder
- $15\frac{3}{5}$ ← As a fraction
- 15.6 ← As a decimal

Long Division

When a division sum has a double-digit divisor, you may need to use long division.

Example

Calculate 477 ÷ 15

1. 477 ÷ 15. There are 30 lots of 15 in 477. Record the 3 in the tens column above the line. 30 × 15 = 450. Subtract this from 477 and put the answer below.

```
          3
   15 | 4 7 7
      - 4 5 0  ← 15 × 30
        2 7
```

2. 27 ÷ 15. There is 1 lot of 15 in 27. Record the 1 above the line in the units column. 12 is left over. 12 cannot be divided by 15 so there is a remainder of 12.

```
          3 1
   15 | 4 7 7
      - 4 5 0  ← 15 × 30
        2 7
      -   1 5  ← 15 × 1
      r   1 2
```

3. 477 ÷ 15 = 31r12

   To find a decimal answer you need to put a decimal point on the answer line and bring down a zero to the remainder.

   120 ÷ 15 = 8

```
          3 1 . 8
   15 | 4 7 7 . 0
      - 4 5 0
        2 7
      -   1 5
          1 2 0  ← 15 × 8
      -   1 2 0
              0
```

   477 ÷ 15 = 31.8

Quick Test

Work out these calculations using the 'bus stop' method or long division:

1. 112 ÷ 7
2. 198 ÷ 12 (giving your remainder as a decimal)
3. 272 ÷ 16

Key Words

- Divisor
- Most significant digit
- Remainder

Practice Questions

1 What are all the factors of 24? _____

   4 marks

2 What are the common factors of 32 and 48? _____

   5 marks

3 Divide 132 by 5, giving your
   answer with a remainder.

   1 mark

4 Work out 124.5 × 10 mentally. _____

   1 mark

5 What is 6^2? _____

   1 mark

6 Find a prime number between 32 and 40. _____

   1 mark

1 Find three common multiples of 3 and 5. _____

   3 marks

2 What is the product of 6, 8 and 4? _____

   1 mark

3 Divide 174 by 12, giving your
   answer with a fraction.

   1 mark

4 Work out 13.65 ÷ 100 mentally. _____

   1 mark

5 What is 2^3? _____

   1 mark

6 Work out 38 × 29
   using a written method.

   1 mark

1 Find the prime factors of 30. _____

   1 mark

2 Work out 234 × 16
   using a written method.

   1 mark

3 What is 5^3? _____

   1 mark

4 Divide 248 by 16, giving your
   answer as a decimal.

   1 mark

Review Questions

1 Find the number bonds to 100 for:

a) 26 _____ b) 17 _____ c) 52 _____
3 marks

2 Work out 599 + 64 mentally. _____
1 mark

3 Work out 702 – 35 mentally. _____
1 mark

4 Find the number bonds to 1000 for:

a) 376 _____ b) 745 _____ c) 28 _____
3 marks

5 Work out 70 + 180 mentally. _____
1 mark

6 Work out 230 – 90 mentally. _____
1 mark

7 157 + _____ = 190
1 mark

8 Which estimate is nearest for 68 + 71? Tick the correct answer.

240 ☐   140 ☐   130 ☐
1 mark

9 Work out 2371 + 3268
using a written method.
1 mark

PS 10 Jo spends £23.54 and Saira spends £12.56.

How much do the girls spend altogether?

_____
1 mark

11 Work out 1984 – 1167
using a written method.
1 mark

PS 12 I earned £34.82 from helping at home.
I spent £15.45 on a new bag.

How much money do I have left? _____
1 mark

PS 13 Colleen spends £23.14 on clothes
and £5.45 on a new pencil case.

How much change will she get from £50? _____
1 mark

Fractions

- Understand simple fractions
- Find fractions of amounts
- Simplify fractions
- Understand equivalent fractions
- Order fractions

Simple Fractions

A fraction is a part of a whole. The number at the bottom tells you how many parts are in the whole. This is called the **denominator**. The number at the top tells you how many parts of the whole you have. This is called the **numerator**.

Example

$\frac{5}{8}$ means that something is divided into eight parts and you have five of these eight parts.

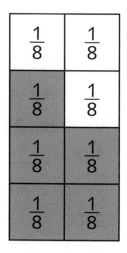

Finding Fractions of Amounts

To find a fraction of an amount, divide the amount by the denominator and multiply by the numerator.

Example

Find $\frac{3}{4}$ of 24.

$24 \div 4 = 6$ ← Divide by denominator.

$6 \times 3 = 18$ ← Multiply by numerator.

$\frac{3}{4}$ of 24 = 18

Simplifying Fractions

You can simplify fractions to make them easier to work with and to find **equivalent fractions**.

You simplify by dividing the numerator and the denominator by the same number.

Example

$\frac{5}{15}$ and $\frac{1}{3}$ are equivalent fractions.

$$\frac{5}{15} \overset{\div 5}{\underset{\div 5}{=}} \frac{1}{3}$$

Comparing and Ordering Fractions

It is easy to order fractions with the same **denominator**.
The fraction with the lowest numerator will be the smallest.

Example

Put these three fractions in order:

$\frac{5}{8}$ $\frac{1}{8}$ $\frac{3}{8}$ ⟶ smallest $\frac{1}{8}$ $\frac{3}{8}$ $\frac{5}{8}$ largest

Key Point

The lowest common denominator is the lowest common multiple of two or more numbers.

You may be asked to order fractions that have different denominators. To do this you need to find the **lowest common denominator** for all the fractions.

Example

Put these three fractions in order:

$\frac{3}{4}$ $\frac{5}{8}$ $\frac{1}{2}$

Before you can put these three fractions in order, you need to find the lowest common denominator for 8, 4 and 2.

8 is the lowest common denominator.

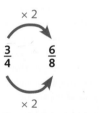

$\times 2$
$\frac{3}{4}$ $\frac{6}{8}$ $\frac{5}{8}$ $\frac{1}{2}$ $\frac{4}{8}$
$\times 2$ $\times 4$

$\times 4$

> You must convert all the fractions into eighths because 8 is the lowest common denominator.

Now you can order them:

$\frac{1}{2}$ $\frac{5}{8}$ $\frac{3}{4}$

smallest ⟶ largest

Quick Test

1. Simplify: **a)** $\frac{8}{24}$ **b)** $\frac{10}{15}$ **c)** $\frac{18}{15}$
2. Which fraction from the list below is equivalent to $\frac{3}{18}$?
   $\frac{1}{3}$ $\frac{3}{5}$ $\frac{1}{6}$ $\frac{6}{12}$
3. Order these fractions from smallest to largest:
   $\frac{2}{12}$ $\frac{3}{6}$ $\frac{1}{4}$ $\frac{2}{3}$

Key Words

- Denominator
- Numerator
- Equivalent fraction
- Lowest common denominator

Adding, Subtracting, Multiplying and Dividing Fractions

- Add and subtract fractions with the same denominator
- Add fractions with different denominators
- Multiply and divide fractions

Adding and Subtracting Fractions

Adding and subtracting fractions with the same **denominator** is easy. Simply add or subtract all the **numerators**.

Tip

Remember that you are only adding or subtracting the numerators. The denominator stays the same.

Example 1

$$\frac{3}{10} + \frac{5}{10} = \frac{8}{10}$$

Example 2

$$\frac{6}{8} - \frac{1}{8} = \frac{5}{8}$$

Adding Fractions with Different Denominators

If the denominators are different, you need to find the **lowest common denominator** for both fractions.

Example

$$\frac{1}{5} + \frac{2}{3} =$$

The lowest common denominator of 5 and 3 is 15. You need to convert both fractions to have a denominator of 15.

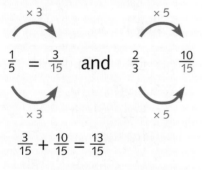

$$\frac{1}{5} = \frac{3}{15} \quad \text{and} \quad \frac{2}{3} = \frac{10}{15}$$

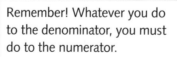

Remember! Whatever you do to the denominator, you must do to the numerator.

$$\frac{1}{5} + \frac{2}{3} = ?$$

$$\frac{3}{15} + \frac{10}{15} = \frac{13}{15}$$

Multiplying Fractions

To multiply fractions you multiply both numerators and then multiply both denominators. You can then simplify your answer by dividing the numerator and the denominator by the same number.

Example

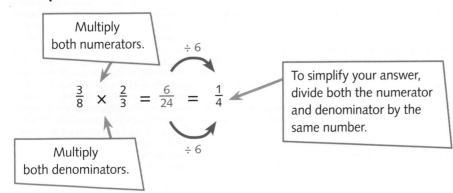

Multiply both numerators.

÷ 6

To simplify your answer, divide both the numerator and denominator by the same number.

$$\frac{3}{8} \times \frac{2}{3} = \frac{6}{24} = \frac{1}{4}$$

Multiply both denominators.

÷ 6

Dividing Fractions

You can divide fractions by **whole numbers**.

Example

Work out $\frac{1}{3} \div 2$

You know that a shape divided into thirds has three parts. If you halve the thirds, you would have six parts.

So, $\frac{1}{3} \div 2 = \frac{1}{6}$

$\frac{1}{3}$ $\frac{1}{3}$ $\frac{1}{3}$

$\frac{1}{6}$ | $\frac{1}{6}$

Quick Test

1. Work out $\frac{2}{12} + \frac{5}{12} + \frac{3}{12}$ and simplify your answer.
2. $\frac{1}{2} \times \frac{1}{4}$
3. $\frac{5}{8} + \frac{3}{4}$
4. $\frac{1}{4} \div 2$

Key Word

• Whole number

Decimal Fractions

- Understand the decimal number line
- Calculate decimals
- Order decimals
- Round decimals

Decimal Number Line

You can divide a 0 – 1 number line into 10 equal parts to create a decimal number line. Each part is $\frac{1}{10}$ (one-tenth) or 0.1.

You can divide each $\frac{1}{10}$ into 10 equal parts. Each part is $\frac{1}{100}$ (one-hundredth) or 0.01.

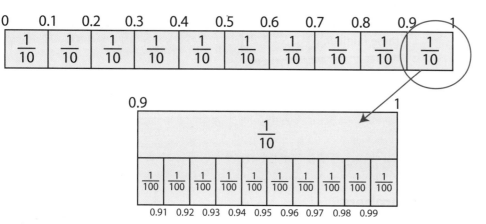

> ### Tip
>
> You can remember that $\frac{1}{10}$ is 0.1 and $\frac{1}{100}$ is 0.01 because 0.1 is 10 backwards and 0.01 is 100 backwards.

Calculating Decimals

To convert a fraction to a decimal, you divide the numerator by the denominator.

Example 1

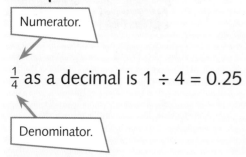

Numerator.

$\frac{1}{4}$ as a decimal is $1 \div 4 = 0.25$

Denominator.

Example 2

$\frac{3}{5}$ as a decimal is $3 \div 5 = 0.6$

Ordering Decimals

You can order decimals in the same way as for **whole numbers**.

Example

0.347   0.354   0.35   0.356

All the numbers have a 3 in the tenths column, so you need to look at the hundredths column.

0.347   0.354   0.350   0.356

All these numbers have a 5 as the hundredths, so you need to look at the thousandths column to order them.

So the correct order is 0.347, 0.35, 0.354, 0.356

Tip

Before you start ordering your decimals, add some zeros to give them all the same number of digits, e.g. if the other numbers have three **decimal places**, change 0.35 to 0.350.

Rounding Decimals

The rules for rounding decimals are the same as those for rounding whole numbers.

Example

To round 3.485 to the nearest whole number, look at the tenths digit. It's a 4 so round down to 3.

To round 3.485 to one decimal place, look at the hundredths digit. It's an 8 so round up to 3.5.

To round 3.485 to two decimal places, look at the thousandths digit. It's a 5 so round up to 3.49.

Rounding decimals is easy!

Quick Test

1. Convert $\frac{35}{100}$ to a decimal.
2. Round 3.61 to one decimal place.
3. Order these decimals from smallest to largest:
   8.43   8.4   8.57   8.55

Key Word

• Decimal place

Improper Fractions and Mixed Numbers

* Recognise improper fractions
* Recognise mixed numbers
* Convert mixed numbers and improper fractions

Improper Fractions

Sometimes when you add fractions you get a 'top heavy' fraction where the numerator is greater than the denominator.

This is an **improper fraction** and its value is greater than 1.

Example

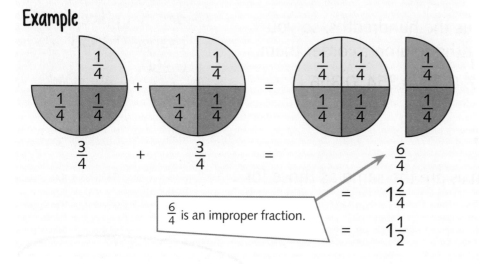

$$\frac{3}{4} + \frac{3}{4} = \frac{6}{4}$$

$\frac{6}{4}$ is an improper fraction.

$$= 1\frac{2}{4}$$
$$= 1\frac{1}{2}$$

Tip

Always simplify $\frac{2}{4}$ to $\frac{1}{2}$.

Mixed Numbers

The example above shows that $\frac{6}{4}$ equals $1\frac{1}{2}$. $1\frac{1}{2}$ is a **mixed number** because it is made up of a whole number and a fraction.

Example

Here you have one apple and half an apple, so you say $1\frac{1}{2}$ apples.

Converting Improper Fractions and Mixed Numbers

You can convert mixed numbers to improper fractions.

Example

Convert $2\frac{1}{3}$ to an improper fraction.

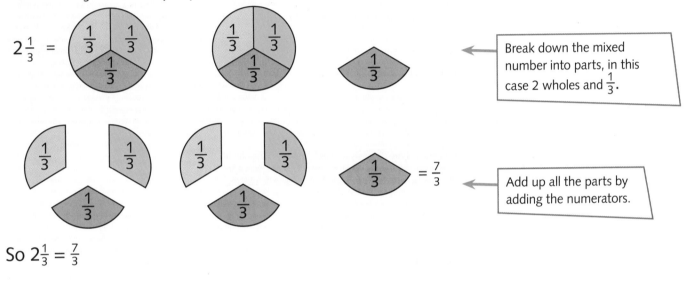

$2\frac{1}{3} =$

Break down the mixed number into parts, in this case 2 wholes and $\frac{1}{3}$.

$= \frac{7}{3}$

Add up all the parts by adding the numerators.

So $2\frac{1}{3} = \frac{7}{3}$

To convert improper fractions to mixed numbers, divide the numerator by the denominator.

Divide the top by the bottom.

Example

Convert $\frac{8}{5}$ to a mixed number.

$\frac{8}{5} = 8 \div 5$

$\quad = 1r3$

$\quad = 1\frac{3}{5}$

Quick Test

1. Convert $2\frac{1}{4}$ to an improper fraction.
2. Convert $\frac{12}{7}$ to a mixed number.

Key Words

- Improper fraction
- Mixed number

Percentages

- Understand and recognise percentages
- Find percentages of amounts

Percentages

Percent means 'number of parts per hundred'. For example, 32% means 32 parts of 100 or $\frac{32}{100}$.

Converting fractions to percentages allows you to compare them.

You need to know the decimals and percentages for these fractions:

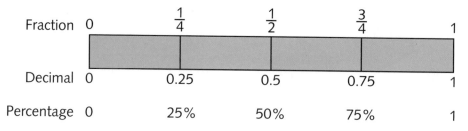

Fraction	0	$\frac{1}{4}$	$\frac{1}{2}$	$\frac{3}{4}$	1
Decimal	0	0.25	0.5	0.75	1
Percentage	0	25%	50%	75%	1

To find a percentage from a fraction:

- divide the numerator by the denominator
- then multiply the answer by 100.

Example

Achal scored $\frac{48}{64}$ in a recent test.

Peter scored $\frac{63}{90}$ in his test.

Who had the better score?

Achal	Peter
$48 \div 64 = 0.75$	$63 \div 90 = 0.70$
$0.75 \times 100 = \mathbf{75\%}$	$0.70 \times 100 = \mathbf{70\%}$
Achal scored 75%	**Peter scored 70%**

Achal scored 75% so he had the better score.

Key Point

Percent means 'parts per hundred'.

Finding Percentages of Amounts

Problems, especially those including money, often ask you to find percentages of amounts.

Example

Find 15% of 64.

It helps to find 10% first:

$64 \times \frac{10}{100} = 6.4$

10% = 6.4

Now that you have found 10%, you can halve it to find 5%:

5% of 64 = 3.2

Add 10% and 5% together to find 15%:

15% of 64 = 6.4 + 3.2

15% of 64 = 9.6

Tip

From finding 10% you can easily calculate other percentages, e.g. 20% = 6.4 × 2 = 12.8 and 60% = 6.4 × 6 = 38.4

Quick Test

1. Find 80% of 120.
2. Jan scored $\frac{15}{25}$ in Science and $\frac{18}{40}$ in Maths. Which subject did he do best in?
3. What is $\frac{38}{50}$ as a percentage?
4. What is $\frac{1}{4}$ as a percentage?

Key Word

- Percent

Practice Questions

Challenge 1

1   Find $\frac{1}{4}$ of 32. _____

1 mark

2   Find 10% of 26. _____

1 mark

3   Convert these fractions to decimals and percentages.
    (You can use a calculator.)

$\frac{1}{4}$ _____ _____ $\frac{25}{75}$ _____ _____ $\frac{45}{90}$ _____ _____

3 marks

4   $\frac{5}{8} + \frac{1}{4} =$ ☐

1 mark

5   Convert $\frac{7}{5}$ into a mixed number. _____

1 mark

6   Order these decimals from smallest to largest:

0.65   0.56   0.61   0.6

_____

1 mark

Challenge 2

1   Find $\frac{3}{4}$ of 48. _____

1 mark

2   Find 30% of 62. _____

1 mark

3   Convert these fractions to decimals and give your answer to 2 decimal places. (You can use a calculator.)

$\frac{24}{96}$ _____ $\frac{17}{85}$ _____ $\frac{51}{68}$ _____

3 marks

4   $\frac{2}{7} + \frac{3}{14} =$ ☐

1 mark

5   Convert $\frac{18}{8}$ into a mixed number, simplifying
    the fraction to its simplest form.   _____

1 mark

Challenge 3

1   Find $\frac{5}{8}$ of 64. _____

1 mark

2   Find 65% of 80. _____

1 mark

3   $\frac{5}{7} + \frac{1}{5} =$ ☐

1 mark

4   What is $3\frac{3}{8}$ as an improper fraction? _____

1 mark

5   Order these from smallest to largest:

$\frac{4}{12}$ $\frac{5}{6}$ $1\frac{1}{3}$ $\frac{1}{4}$ _____

1 mark

Review Questions

PS 1 Peter has three digit cards. He picks up a 5, an 8 and a 2. What is his answer if he multiplies the numbers on his three cards?

_____

1 mark

2 List all the prime numbers between 0 and 20.

_____

4 marks

PS 3 Ciara has 34 boxes of cards. She has 56 cards in each box.

How many cards does she have altogether?

_____

1 mark

4 What are the prime factors of 42? _____

1 mark

5 $4^3 =$ _____

1 mark

6 A teacher shares 213 chocolate bars among 15 children. How many bars does each child get?
(Give your remainder as a decimal.)

1 mark

7 Alan has 112 eggs. He puts 7 in each box.

How many boxes does he fill? _____

1 mark

8 Work out 3.547:

a) × 10 _____   b) × 100 _____   c) × 1000 _____

3 marks

9 Work out 1659:

a) ÷ 10 _____   b) ÷ 100 _____   c) ÷ 1000 _____

3 marks

10 What are the common factors of 15 and 30?

_____

1 mark

11 Christie has some wooden bricks 3.8 cm long. If she puts 24 bricks end to end, how long is her line of bricks in cm?

_____

1 mark

Units of Measurement

- Be able to use different measures
- Convert measures
- Understand imperial measures

Different Measures and their Units

Different objects are measured in many different units.

Some units (in blue) are not often used these days. They were part of an **imperial** system. Today we use a **metric** system for most measures.

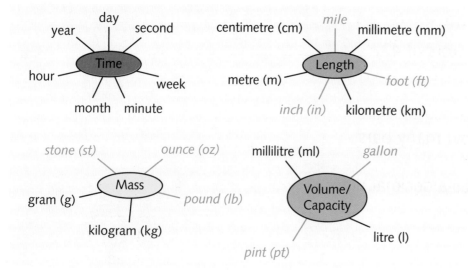

Converting Measures

You can use your skills in multiplying and dividing by 10, 100 and 1000 to convert all metric measures.

Example 1

Length

There are 10 mm in 1 cm; 100 cm in 1 m; and 1000 m in 1 km:

- 3.456 km = 3456 m (× 1000)
  6543 m = 6.543 km (÷ 1000)
- 3 m = 300 cm (× 100)
  345 cm = 3.45 m (÷ 100)
- 34 cm = 340 mm (× 10)
  65 mm = 6.5 cm (÷ 10)

Key Point

When converting lengths:
- multiply or divide by 1000 to convert between m and km
- multiply or divide by 100 to convert between cm and m
- multiply or divide by 10 to convert between mm and cm.

Example 2

Mass

5 kg = 5000 g (× 1000)   273 g = 0.273 kg (÷ 1000)

Volume/Capacity

1 l = 1000 ml (× 1000)   45 ml = 0.045 l (÷ 1000)

Imperial Measures

We stopped using most imperial measures many years ago but you may still come across them, e.g. in a recipe book and on road signs. It can help to know roughly what their values are in the metric system.

Length

1 inch = around 2.5 cm

1 foot = around 30 cm

1 mile = around 1.6 km

Mass

1 ounce (oz) = around 30 g

1 pound (lb) = around 0.5 kg

1 stone = around 6.5 kg

Volume/Capacity

1 pint = around 0.5 litre

1 gallon = around 4.5 litres

> **Tip**
>
> It may help to remember that 30 cm (about 1 foot) is the length of a school ruler.

Quick Test

1. What is 35 cm in mm?
2. How many litres is 254 ml?
3. What is 3.45 kg in grams?
4. How many km is 5 miles?

Key Words

- Imperial
- Metric
- Length
- Mass
- Volume/Capacity

Perimeter and Area

- Calculate the perimeter of regular shapes
- Calculate the perimeter of a rectangle
- Calculate the perimeter of composite shapes
- Calculate the area of a rectangle

Calculating the Perimeter of Regular Shapes

The **perimeter** of a shape is the distance around the outside of a shape. If you know the length of one side, you can use your knowledge of regular shapes to calculate the perimeter.

Example

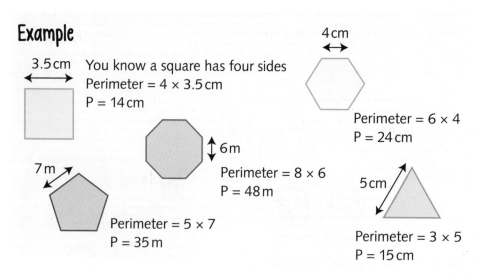

3.5 cm You know a square has four sides
Perimeter = 4 × 3.5 cm
P = 14 cm

4 cm
Perimeter = 6 × 4
P = 24 cm

6 m
Perimeter = 8 × 6
P = 48 m

7 m
Perimeter = 5 × 7
P = 35 m

5 cm
Perimeter = 3 × 5
P = 15 cm

Tip

Think of a **perimeter** fence around an animal enclosure.

Calculating the Perimeter of a Rectangle

The perimeter of this rectangle can be calculated as:

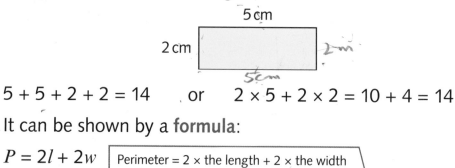

5 cm

2 cm

5 + 5 + 2 + 2 = 14   or   2 × 5 + 2 × 2 = 10 + 4 = 14

It can be shown by a **formula**:

$P = 2l + 2w$ | Perimeter = 2 × the length + 2 × the width

Calculating the Perimeter of Composite Shapes

To calculate the perimeter of a **composite shape**, you need to calculate the lengths of all the sides.

Example

You can use the information you have to calculate the lengths of the two missing sides:

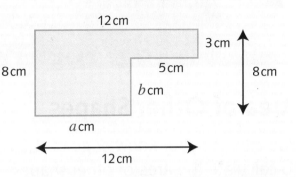

$12 - a = 5$, so $a = 7\,\text{cm}$
$8 - b = 3$, so $b = 5\,\text{cm}$

Perimeter $= 12 + 3 + 5 + 5 + 7 + 8 = 40\,\text{cm}$

Calculating the Area of a Rectangle

The **area** of a shape is the size of the flat surface it takes up. Area is recorded as square units or units². The simplest way to calculate area is to **count** squares.

Example

A carpet is 4 m long and 3 m wide.

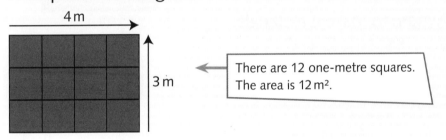

There are 12 one-metre squares. The area is 12 m².

You can also **calculate** the area of a rectangle by multiplying the length by the width.

Area = length × width

$A = l \times w$

Write this as a formula.

The area of the rectangle above can be calculated as
$A = 4 \times 3 = 12\,\text{m}^2$

Key Point

Two rectangles can have the same area ($A = l \times w$) but different perimeters, e.g.

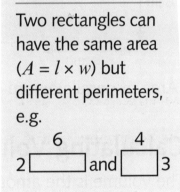

Quick Test

1. One side of a regular hexagon measures 5 cm. What is the perimeter of the shape?
2. Calculate the area of a rectangle that is 6 cm long and 4 cm wide.

Key Words

- Perimeter
- Formula
- Composite shape
- Area

Area, Volume and Money

- Calculate the area of other shapes
- Calculate volume
- Work with money

Area of Other Shapes

You can use your knowledge of squares and rectangles to calculate the area of other shapes.

Example

To calculate the area of a triangle, you can put two triangles together to make a rectangle as shown opposite.

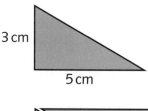

You can use $A = l \times w$ to calculate the area of the rectangle, then divide by 2 to find the area of the triangle.

Area of triangle = $(5 \times 3) \div 2 = 7.5 \, cm^2$

You can reorganise this **parallelogram** to make a rectangle.

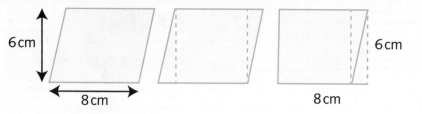

Area of parallelogram = $8 \times 6 = 48 \, cm^2$

Calculating Volume

The volume is the amount of space an object takes up. Volume is measured as **units³**.

Example

Imagine this cuboid is made from 1 cm cubes.

You can calculate the volume by counting the 1 cm cubes. There are 12×1 cm cubes.

$V = 12 \, cm^3$

You can also use the formula:

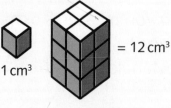

Volume = length × width × height

$V = l \times w \times h$ $V = 2 \times 2 \times 3 = 12 \, cm^3$

> **Tip**
>
> Count the 1 cm cubes as layers from the top down to work out the volume of a cuboid.

Money

Money is either measured in pounds (£) or pence (p). There are 100p in £1. Amounts of money are written as £00.00.

- Convert £ to p by **× 100**, so £5.67 = 567p
- Convert p to £ by **÷ 100**, so 306p = £3.06

To order, add or subtract money convert it all to the same unit, all in £ or all in p.

Example 1

Order these amounts of money from smallest to largest:

£3.67   36p   £36.70   376p

First, change all the amounts to £:

£3.67   £0.36   £36.70   £3.76

Then order them from smallest to largest:

£0.36   £3.67   £3.76   £36.70

smallest   36p   £3.67   376p   £36.70 largest

Example 2

Add these amounts of money: £45.55 + 324p

1. First, change all the amounts to £:
   £45.55 + £3.24

2. Then, add the amounts together:
   = £48.79

Quick Test

1. What is the area of this triangle?

   12 cm

   6 cm

2. Calculate the volume of a brick measuring 3 cm long, 5 cm wide and 6 cm high.
3. What is £567.43 in pence?

Key Words

- Parallelogram
- Units³

Time

- Be able to tell analogue and digital time
- Be able to tell 12- and 24-hour time
- Know weeks, months and years
- Calculate time intervals using number lines

Analogue and Digital Time

Clocks with hands are called **analogue** clocks.

The clock face is split into 12 hours and 60 minutes. The minute hand (the longer one) tells you how many minutes past or to the hour it is and the hour hand (the shorter one) tells you what hour it is near.

Digital clocks have no hands. They use digits past the hour.

If it was 20 to 9, the digital time would be recorded as 8:40. You use **a.m.** to show that it's the morning and **p.m.** to show that it's the afternoon or evening. Any time after 12 midnight is a.m. and any time after 12 noon (midday) is p.m.

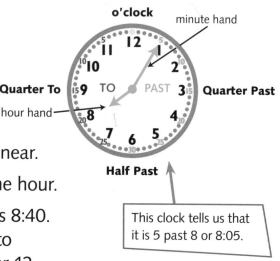

This clock tells us that it is 5 past 8 or 8:05.

12- and 24-Hour Clocks

Because a clock face only has 12 hours on it, you need to use a.m. and p.m. to tell if it is morning or afternoon. **24-hour** clocks don't start at 1 o'clock again after lunch. They continue counting up to 24. 24-hour time is recorded as four digits with the hours and minutes separated by a colon (:).

Key Point

24-hour clocks don't need to use a.m. and p.m.

Example

Quarter past four in the afternoon would be recorded as 4.15 p.m. in 12-hour time and 16:15 in 24-hour time.

12-hour time	24-hour time	12-hour time	24-hour time
12 midnight	00:00	12 noon	12:00
1 a.m.	01:00	1 p.m.	13:00
11 a.m.	11.00	11 p.m.	23:00

Key Point

There is no time recorded as 24:00. After 23:59 it goes to 00:00.

Weeks, Months and Years

There are 60 seconds in one minute and 60 minutes in one hour. There are 24 hours in one day.

There are seven days in a week and 14 days in a **fortnight**. In a year there are 12 months or 52 weeks or 365 days. Once every four years there is a **leap year** and there is an extra day (29 February).

Time Problems

You can use number lines to help solve time problems.

Example

Sameera gets on a bus at 3.45 p.m. The journey takes 35 minutes. What time does Sameera get off?

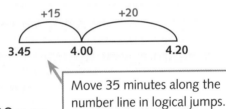

Move 35 minutes along the number line in logical jumps.

Sameera gets off the bus at 4.20 p.m.

Sometimes you need to work out the time interval.

Example

Jo puts her cake in the oven at 5.40 p.m. She takes it out at 7.10 p.m. How long was the cake in the oven?

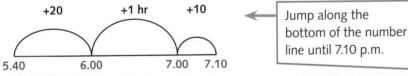

Jump along the bottom of the number line until 7.10 p.m.

Jo's cake was in the oven for 1 hour and 30 minutes.

Quick Test

1. What is 7.35 p.m. in 24-hour time?
2. How many minutes are there in three hours?
3. Aiden's birthday is on 4 August. He had his party one week before. What date did he have his party?

Key Words

- Analogue
- Digital
- a.m.
- p.m.
- 24-hour
- Fortnight
- Leap year

Practice Questions

PS Problem-solving questions

1　Convert:

　　a) 25 cm to mm _____　　b) 1260 m to km _____

　　　　　　　　　　　　　　　　　　　　　　　　　　　　　　　　2 marks

2　Calculate the area and perimeter of this rectangle:

6 cm

4 cm

Area = _____ cm²

Perimeter = _____ cm

2 marks

3　Convert 19:45 to 12-hour time. _____

1 mark

PS 4　Add 345p + £2 and give your answer in £. _____

1 mark

1　Convert:

　　a) 645 ml to l _____　　b) 4.126 kg to g _____

2 marks

2　Calculate the area and perimeter of this rectangle:

90 cm

80 cm

Area = _____ cm²

Perimeter = _____ cm

2 marks

PS 3　One side of a regular pentagon measures 8 cm.

　　What is the perimeter of the shape?　　_____ cm

1 mark

PS 4　Chloe came back from a fortnight's holiday on 12 July.

　　On what date did she go on holiday? _____

1 mark

PS 1　The perimeter of the rectangle is 29 m. What is the width of the rectangle?

12 m

?

_____ m

1 mark

2　What is the volume of this cuboid?

8 cm

3 cm

2 cm

_____ cm³

1 mark

3　Convert 23 467 m to km.

　　Round your answer to one decimal place. _____

1 mark

4　What is the area of this triangle? _____ cm²　　4 cm

8.5 cm

1 mark

Review Questions

1 What is $\frac{2}{7}$ of 42? _____

1 mark

2 Express $\frac{24}{40}$ in its simplest form. ☐

1 mark

3 Which fraction below is equivalent to $\frac{2}{3}$? Tick the correct answer.

$\frac{5}{20}$ ☐ $\frac{5}{16}$ ☐ $\frac{16}{24}$ ☐ $\frac{8}{40}$ ☐

1 mark

4 $\frac{5}{11} + \frac{3}{11} =$ ☐

1 mark

5 What is half of $\frac{1}{8}$? ☐

1 mark

6 $\frac{1}{6} \times \frac{1}{5} =$ ☐

1 mark

PS 7 Sophia and Jacob were eating pizzas. Sophia ate $\frac{7}{10}$ of her pizza and Jacob ate $\frac{4}{5}$ of his pizza.

Who ate the most? _____

1 mark

8 Order these decimals from largest to smallest:

3.24   2.35   3.2   2.34   3.25

_____

4 marks

9 Round 23.71 to the nearest:

a) $\frac{1}{10}$ _____ b) whole number _____

2 marks

10 Change $\frac{12}{5}$ into a mixed number. _____

1 mark

11 Change $3\frac{1}{4}$ into an improper fraction. ☐

1 mark

12 James got 75% in a test. What is 75% as a fraction and a decimal?

Fraction: ☐   Decimal: _____

1 mark

13 Find 80% of 40. _____

1 mark

Angles, Lines and Circles

- Recognise obtuse, acute and right angles
- Recognise perpendicular and parallel lines
- Measure circles

Obtuse, Acute and Right Angles

Angles are measured in **degrees** °. You can measure angles with a protractor.

A **right angle** measures 90° and is shown as:

If you turn around fully once, you will have turned through 360°. Because there are four right angles in a whole turn, if you turn $\frac{1}{4}$ of a turn you turn 90°.

A $\frac{1}{2}$ turn = 180°.   A $\frac{3}{4}$ turn = 270°.

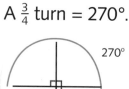

270°

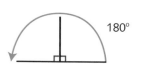

180°

A turn can be **clockwise** or **anti-clockwise**.

Here are some other types of angle:
- **Acute** angles are less than 90°.
- **Obtuse** angles are greater than 90° but less than 180°.
- **Reflex** angles are more than 180° but less than 360°.

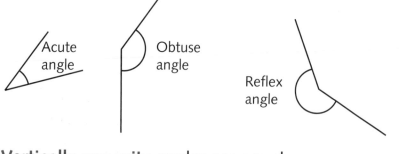

Acute angle

Obtuse angle

Reflex angle

- **Vertically opposite** angles are equal.

  So $a = b$ and $c = d$.

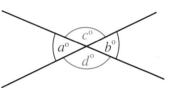

Perpendicular and Parallel Lines

A **perpendicular** line lies at 90° to another line.

Perpendicular

90°

Parallel lines stay the same distance apart and never touch.

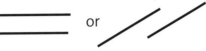 or

Circles

Circles can be described by **diameter**, **radius** and **circumference**:

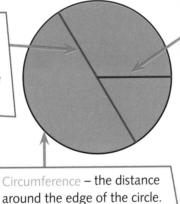

Diameter (*d*) – the distance, through the centre, across the circle (twice the radius).

Radius (*r*) – the distance from the edge to the centre of the circle (half the diameter).

Circumference – the distance around the edge of the circle.

$d = 2r$ or $r = \frac{1}{2}d$

Tip

Think of a train track. Train tracks have parallel lines.

Key Words

- Degrees
- Right angle
- Clockwise
- Anti-clockwise
- Acute
- Obtuse
- Reflex
- Vertically opposite
- Angle on a straight line
- Perpendicular
- Parallel
- Diameter
- Radius
- Circumference

Quick Test

1. If I turn around $1\frac{1}{2}$ times, how many degrees have I turned? *540°*
2. Which angles are acute? Which angles are obtuse?
   a   b   c   d   e
3. This is line 'x'. _____
   Which line is **a)** parallel to x? **b)** perpendicular to x?
   a   b   c   d

57

2-D Shapes

- Know regular and irregular shapes
- Recognise triangles and quadrilaterals
- Find missing angles and sides

Regular and Irregular Shapes

Shapes are **regular** if their sides are the same length.
Irregular shapes have sides of different lengths.

All the interior angles of regular shapes are equal.

Regular Shapes	Irregular Shapes
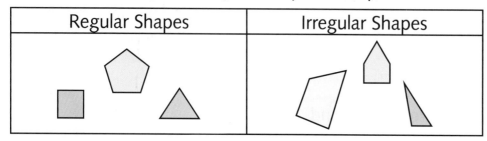	

Triangles and Quadrilaterals

There are three types of triangles:

Equilateral triangles have three equal sides and three equal angles (all 60°).

Isosceles triangles have two equal sides and two equal angles.

Scalene triangles have no equal sides and all their angles are different.

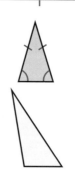

Make sure you know the properties of these **quadrilaterals** (shapes with four sides):

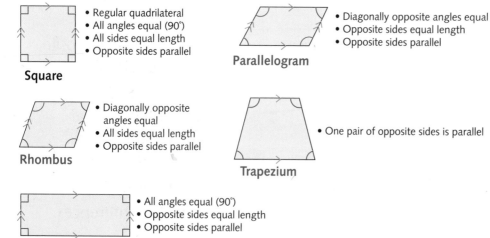

- Regular quadrilateral
- All angles equal (90°)
- All sides equal length
- Opposite sides parallel

Square

- Diagonally opposite angles equal
- Opposite sides equal length
- Opposite sides parallel

Parallelogram

- Diagonally opposite angles equal
- All sides equal length
- Opposite sides parallel

Rhombus

- One pair of opposite sides is parallel

Trapezium

- All angles equal (90°)
- Opposite sides equal length
- Opposite sides parallel

Rectangle

The interior angles of every triangle always add up to 180° and the interior angles of all quadrilaterals add up to 360°. You can use these known facts to calculate missing angles.

Example 1

What does angle a measure?

$94° + 27° + a = 180°$

$a = 180° - (94° + 27°)$

$a = 180° - 121°$

$a = 59°$

Example 2

What are angles x, y and z?

Opposite angles are equal so $y = 110°$

All angles add up to 360° so $x = z = 70°$

You can calculate the total of the interior angles of any regular **polygon** by dividing it into triangles.

Example

This pentagon has been divided into three triangles.

The angles of a triangle total 180°.

So, you can say that the angles of the pentagon = $3 \times 180° = 540°$

Quick Test

1. Calculate the missing angles a and b in this isosceles triangle:

s

solid shapes. They are called 3-D because
dimensions:

ly has two dimensions. You need to know
es come together to make up common

edron

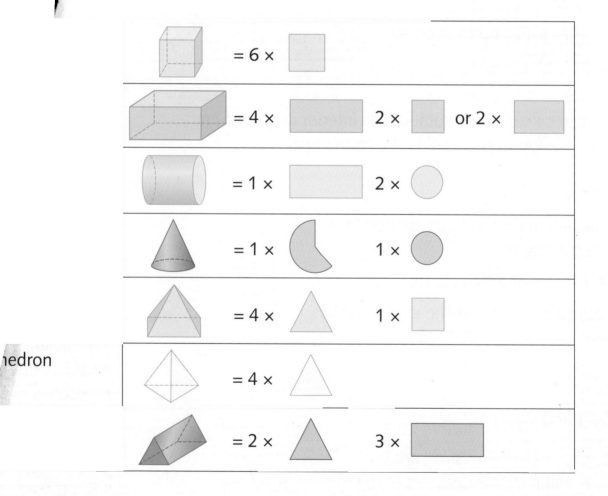

Nets

A **net** of a 3-D shape is the 2-D shape that appears if the 3-D shape is opened up.

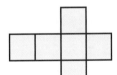
Example

This map is a net of the world. If you cut around it and stuck it together, it would form a sphere.

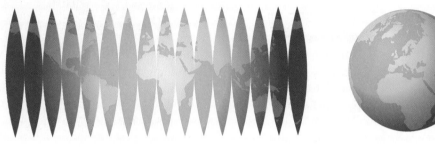

You can create nets of common 3-D shapes by putting together 2-D shapes.

Example

This net is made of six squares. It would fold up to make a cube.

This net is made from two squares and four rectangles. It would fold up to make a cuboid.

Quick Test

1. What 2-D shapes and how many of them would come together to make a pentagonal-based prism?
2. What 3-D shape would this net make?

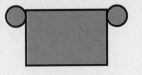

Symmetry

Finding Lines of Symmetry

A shape or object is **symmetrical** if one side is the mirror image of the other.

Example

This plant pot is symmetrical. The dotted line is the **line of symmetry**. Each side is the mirror image of the other.

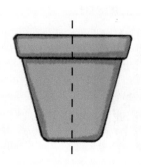

Tip

Imagine folding the image along the line. If it is exactly the same on both sides, it is symmetrical.

Shapes have lines of symmetry:

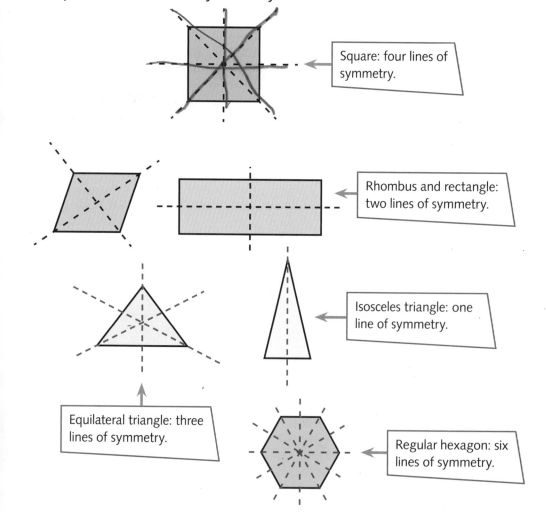

Square: four lines of symmetry.

Rhombus and rectangle: two lines of symmetry.

Isosceles triangle: one line of symmetry.

Equilateral triangle: three lines of symmetry.

Regular hexagon: six lines of symmetry.

Completing Symmetrical Patterns

To complete a symmetrical pattern, you need to reflect it in the line of symmetry.

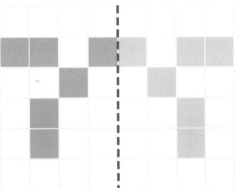

The line of symmetry can be drawn in any direction:

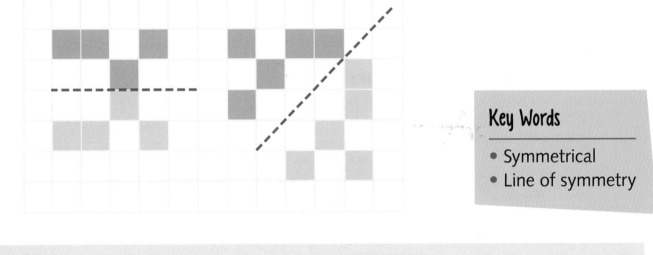

Quick Test

1. Which image, A or B, is the reflection of this pattern?

2. Draw the line of symmetry on this triangle.

Practice Questions

Monday (handwritten)

Challenge 1

1   The radius of a circle is 4.5 cm. What is the diameter? ___9 cm.___   *1 mark*

2   Measure angle x. ___45___   *1 mark*

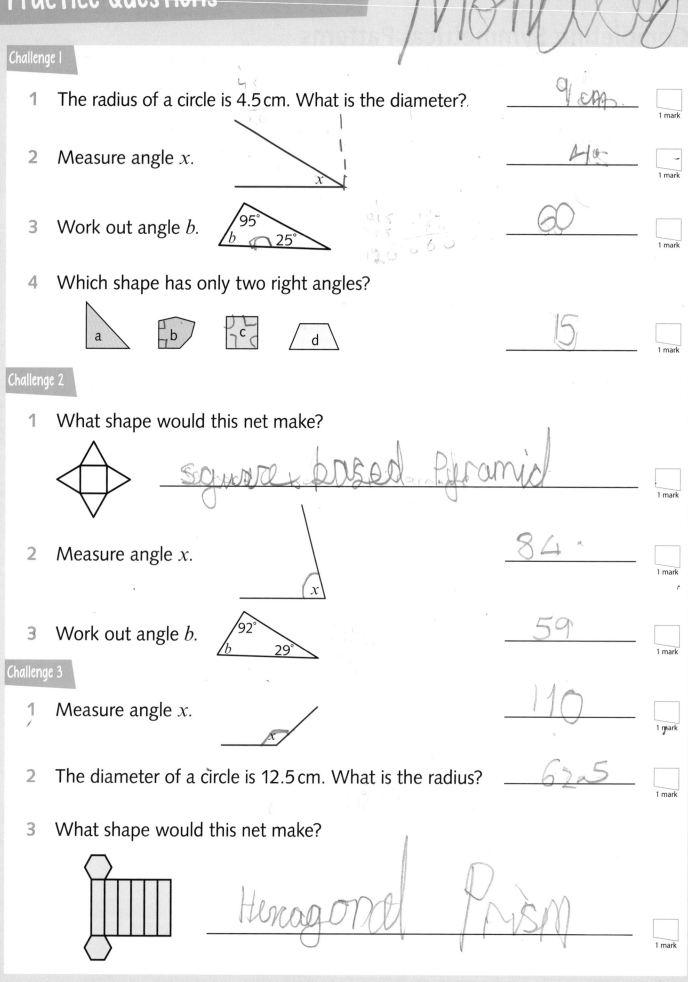

3   Work out angle b. 95° b 25° ___60___   *1 mark*

4   Which shape has only two right angles?

a   b   c   d ___15___   *1 mark*

Challenge 2

1   What shape would this net make? ___square based Pyramid___   *1 mark*

2   Measure angle x. ___84___   *1 mark*

3   Work out angle b. 92° b 29° ___59___   *1 mark*

Challenge 3

1   Measure angle x. ___110___   *1 mark*

2   The diameter of a circle is 12.5 cm. What is the radius? ___6.25___   *1 mark*

3   What shape would this net make? ___Hexagonal Prism___   *1 mark*

PS Problem-solving questions

1 What units would you record the width of your exercise book in? _____ ☐ 1 mark

PS 2 Complete this table, filling in the blanks:

mm	cm	m
35	3.5	0.035
270	27	0.27
3570	357	3.57

6 marks

PS 3 Joshua drank five pints of milk.

Approximately how many litres did he drink? _____2.5_____ l

500
× 5
2500

☐ 1 mark

4 One side of a regular octagon measures 6.5 cm.

What is the perimeter of the shape? _____52_____ cm

6.5
×8
52.0

☐ 1 mark

PS 5 Calculate the perimeter of this shape:

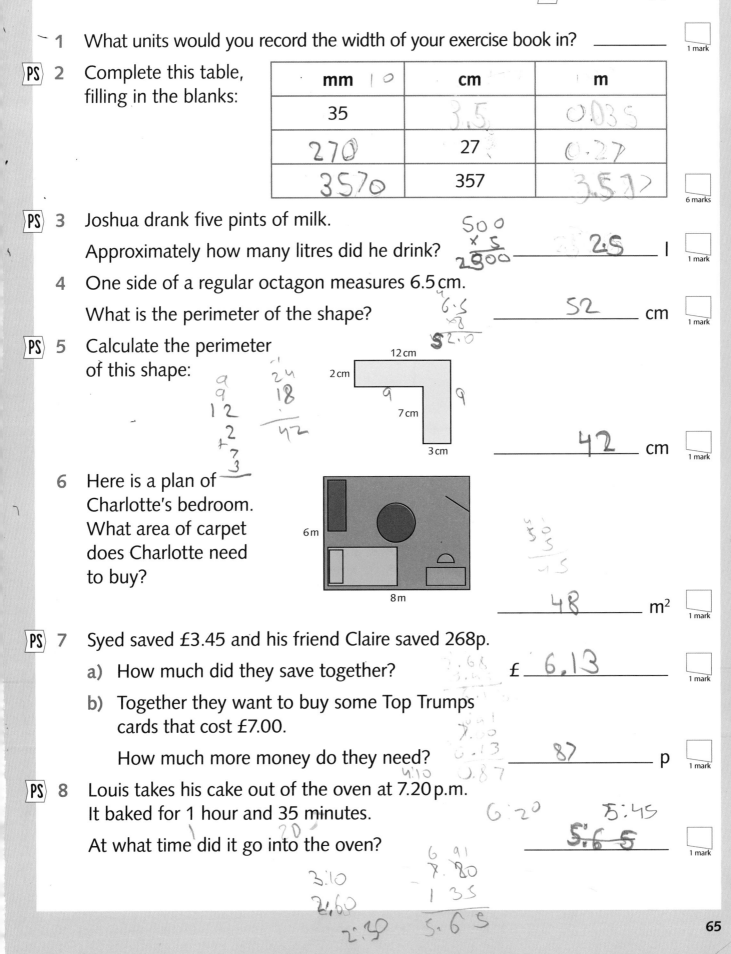

12 cm
2 cm
7 cm
3 cm

a
9
9
1 2
2
+ 7
3

24
18
42

_____42_____ cm

☐ 1 mark

6 Here is a plan of Charlotte's bedroom. What area of carpet does Charlotte need to buy?

6 m

8 m

_____48_____ m²

☐ 1 mark

PS 7 Syed saved £3.45 and his friend Claire saved 268p.

a) How much did they save together? £_____6.13_____

☐ 1 mark

b) Together they want to buy some Top Trumps cards that cost £7.00.

How much more money do they need? _____87_____ p

☐ 1 mark

PS 8 Louis takes his cake out of the oven at 7.20 p.m.
It baked for 1 hour and 35 minutes.

At what time did it go into the oven? _____5.65_____

6:20   5:45
5.65

3:10
2.60
2:50

6 91
7. 80
1 35
5. 6 5

☐ 1 mark

Plotting Points

- Plot points in the first quadrant
- Plot points in four quadrants
- Plot coordinates on a line

Plotting Points in the First Quadrant

Coordinates are the location of a point. They are written as (x, y) where the x coordinate is the distance along the x **axis** and the y coordinate is the distance up the y **axis**.

The point (0,0) is called the **origin**. Points are marked with a dot or small cross.

Example

The point A (3,4) is plotted on the grid.

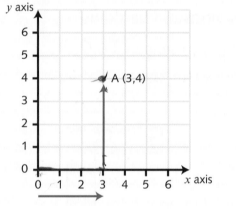

> **Tip**
>
> Remember that the x coordinate comes before the y coordinate because (x,y) is in alphabetical order.

Plotting Points in the Four Quadrants

The grid can be extended past the origin into four **quadrants** to give negative numbers on the axes.

Points are plotted in the same way as for the first quadrant except that the x and y values may be negative. This is called plotting points in four quadrants.

Example

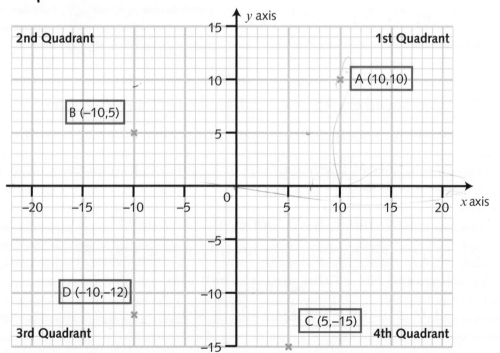

Coordinates on a Line

Knowing the coordinates of points on a line will help you find missing coordinates.

Example

Look at grid A below. Look at the coordinates of the points already plotted: (1,3), (2,3), (3,3), (4,3).

You will notice that the y coordinate is always 3. So, if you plot another point on this line, its y coordinate will be 3.

Look at grid B. Look at the coordinates of the points already plotted: (4,2), (4,3), (4,4), (4,5).

You will notice that the x coordinate is always 4. So, if you plot another point on this line, its x coordinate will be 4.

64

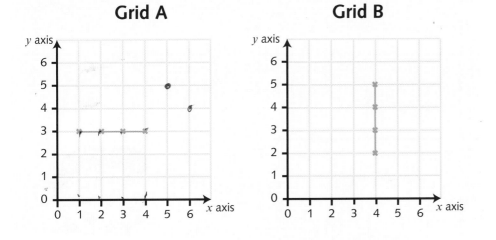

Grid A   **Grid B**

Quick Test

1. What is the horizontal axis called?
2. What are the coordinates of the origin?
3. What are the coordinates of points A, B, C and D?

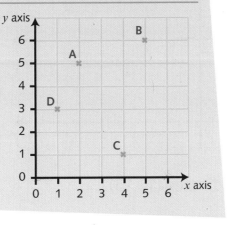

Key Words

- x axis
- y axis
- Origin
- Quadrant

Translation

- Translate points
- Translate shapes

Translating Points

You can move points across and up or down a coordinate grid. This is called **translation**.

When you mark the translated points, you add ' after the letter, for example A', B', C'.

Example

If you move point A (–10,8) 20 units right and 7 units up, what will the coordinates of the new point A' be?

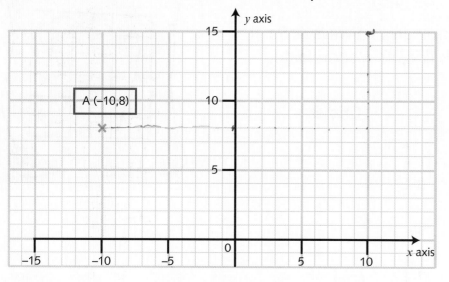

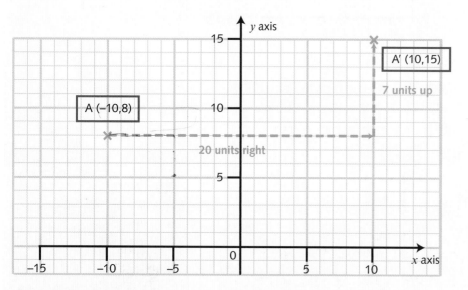

The new point A' has coordinates (10,15).

Key Point

Translated points are recorded as A' to show the point A has moved to a new location.

Translating Shapes

You can translate whole shapes by moving each point in turn.

Example

Translate triangle A 2 squares right and 3 squares up.

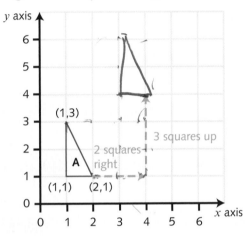

By translating each point of the triangle in turn, you can plot the position of the new triangle A'.

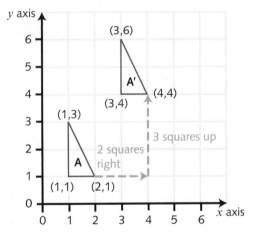

Quick Test

1. If you move a shape up, down or sideways on a coordinate grid, what is it called?
2. On the grid on page 68, if you move point A(–10,8) 5 units right and 3 units down, what are the coordinates of the new point A'?

Reflection

- Reflect points and shapes in the x axis
- Reflect points and shapes in the y axis

Reflecting Points and Shapes in the x Axis

You can use the axes of a coordinate grid as lines to reflect shapes. This is called **reflection**.

A shape can be reflected in the x axis.

Example

Reflect triangle A in the x axis to produce a new triangle A'.

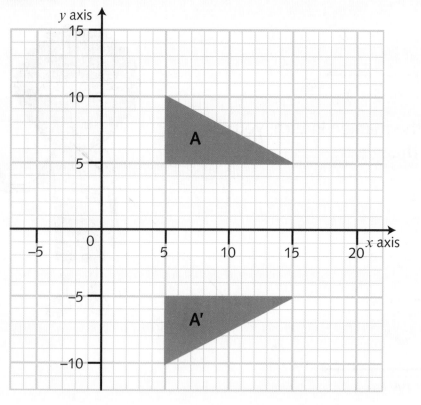

Tip

When reflecting a shape on a grid, imagine that the axis is a mirror line – a bit like symmetry!

The coordinates of the **vertices** of the reflected triangle A' are (5,–10), (5,–5), (15,–5).

The original shape and the **reflected shape** are the same size. The original shape has only changed its position.

The vertices of the reflected shape are the same distance from the x axis as the vertices of the original shape – they are just on the other side of the axis.

Reflecting Points and Shapes in the y Axis

A shape can be reflected in the y axis.

The vertices of the reflected shape are the same distance from the y axis as the vertices of the original shape – again, they are just on the other side of the axis.

Tip

Reflected points can be recorded as A', B', C' or A", B", C", etc. to show that the original shape has changed position.

Example

Reflect triangle A in the y axis to produce a new triangle A".

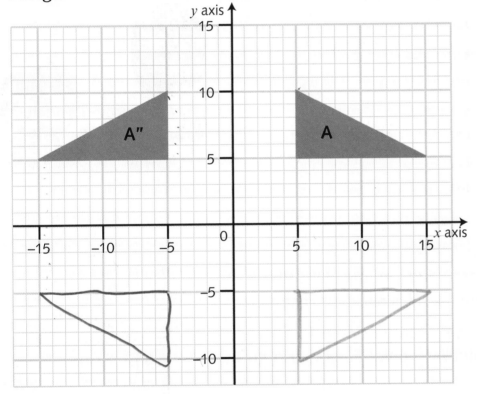

The coordinates of the vertices of the reflected triangle A" are (–5,10), (–5,5), (–15,5).

Quick Test

1. If you use the x or y axis as a mirror line, what is the change in position called?
2. On the grid above, reflect triangle A" in the x axis. Give the coordinates of the vertices of the reflected triangle.

Key Words

- Reflection
- Vertices

Missing Coordinates

• Be able to find missing coordinates

Finding Missing Coordinates

You can find missing coordinates by using your knowledge of shapes.

Example

Shape ABCD is a parallelogram. What are the coordinates of point D?

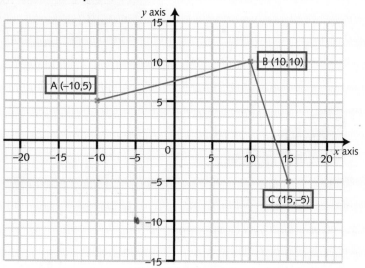

In a parallelogram the opposite sides are **parallel** and of equal length. So, line BC equals and is parallel to line AD.

To get from point B to point C, you go down 15 and along 5. So to go from point A to point D, you also go down 15 and along 5.

Plot point D at (–5,–10).

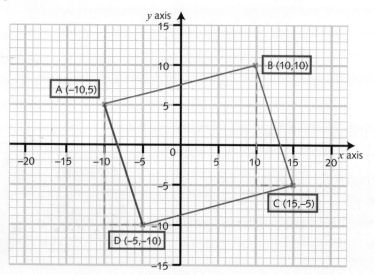

Key Point

Finding missing coordinates is just like translating points.

Unlabelled Axes

Sometimes the axes are not labelled with numbers and there is no grid. However, it's still possible to work out the missing coordinates.

Example

ABCD is a square. What are the coordinates of point D?

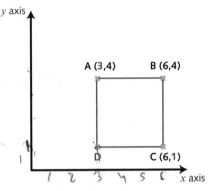

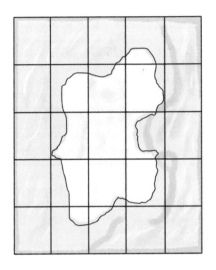

From your knowledge of the **properties** of a square and what you know about coordinates in a line, you know that point D will have the same **x coordinate** as point **A** and the same **y coordinate** as point **C**.

So the coordinates of point D are (3,1).

Quick Test

1. What are the coordinates of points B and D?

2. DEFG is a square. What are the coordinates of point E?

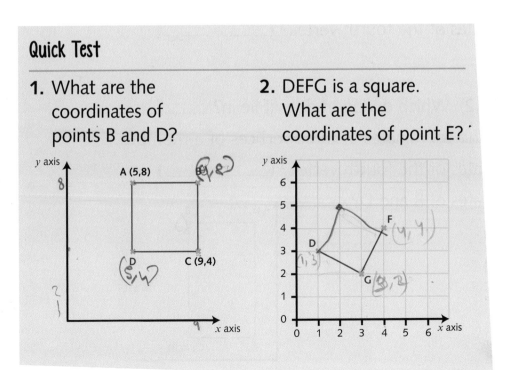

Key Words

- Parallel
- Properties

Practice Questions

H

1 List the coordinates of A, B and C.

A (_2_ , _4_)

B (_4_ , _5_)

C (_6_ , _1_)

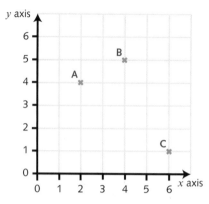

3 marks

2 On the grid paper on page 111, plot triangle A with vertices (3,1), (4,3), (4,1).

3 marks

3 Reflect triangle A in question 2 to A' in the *x* axis and list its new coordinates.

(_3_ , _– 2_) (_4_ , _-2_) (_4_ , _-4_)

3 marks

4 What are the coordinates of the origin? (_0_ , _0_)

1 mark

1 On the grid paper on page 111, plot triangle A with vertices (2,1), (4,–4), (5,0).

3 marks

2 Translate triangle A, in question 1, 4 units left and 2 units down and list the coordinates of A'.

(_-2_ , _-1_) (_0_ , _-6_) (_1_ , _-2_)

3 marks

3 (2,4), (4,4), (4,2) are the coordinates of three vertices of a square.

What are the coordinates of the fourth vertex? (_2_ , _2_)

1 mark

1 Jai plots the point (–3,2). Which quadrant does it lie in? _____2_____

1 mark

2 (3,6), (3,2), (2,4) are the coordinates of three vertices of a rhombus.

What are the coordinates of the fourth vertex? (_8_ , _8_)

1 mark

3 What are the coordinates of B and D?

B (_10_ , _11_)

D (_3_ , _3_)

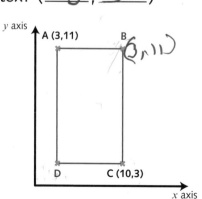

2 marks

Review Questions

1 What are the properties of an isosceles triangle?

_____

2 marks

2 Measure this angle:

_____ x

_____ 1 mark

3 Look at these two shapes:
  Which lines are:
  a) Parallel to line ab?

_____ 1 mark

  b) Perpendicular to ab?

_____ 1 mark

4 A circle has radius 12.8 cm. What is the diameter?

_____ 1 mark

5 What 3-D shape does
  this net make?

_____ 1 mark

6 Calculate angle y.

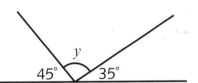

45°   35°

_____ 1 mark

7 Which shape is symmetrical to this one? Tick the correct answer.

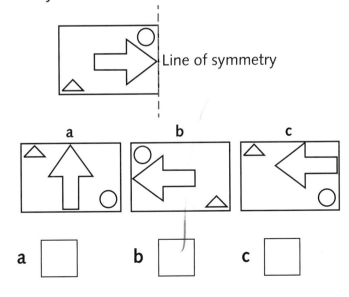

Line of symmetry

a   b   c

a ☐   b ☐   c ☐

1 mark

All Types of Charts

• Recognise and be able to understand pictograms, bar charts, line charts and pie charts

Pictograms

Pictograms use pictures to represent a certain number of something.

Example

This pictogram shows that there are 35 flowers in the garden.

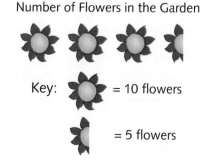

Number of Flowers in the Garden

Key: = 10 flowers

= 5 flowers

Bar Charts

Bar charts also display information (data) and make it easy to compare different amounts. A bar chart should have a title, and titles and labels on the axes.

Example

You can use this bar chart to answer questions such as:
• What is the most popular flavour of crisps?
• How many children like salt and vinegar crisps best?

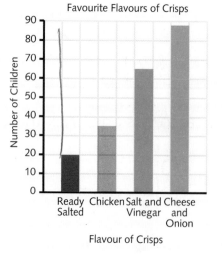

Favourite Flavours of Crisps

Key Point

Bar charts always need to have a title, and titles and labels on the x and y axes.

Line Charts

Line charts are often used to show changes over time. For example, temperature or rainfall readings on weather charts and weight or height changes.

Unlike bar charts, the x **axis** labels on line charts must line up exactly with the grid lines. All the plotted points need to be joined carefully with straight lines.

Example

You can use this line chart to answer questions such as:

- Which month had the highest rainfall?
- What is the difference between the rainfall recorded in April and in December?

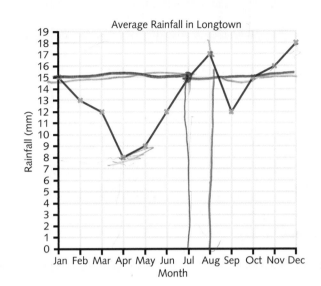

Average Rainfall in Longtown

Pie Charts

Pie charts display information by dividing a circle into different-sized pieces to show each measurement.

Use a **protractor** to draw pie charts. Calculate the angles by finding the measurement as a fraction of the total × 360°.

Example

This table shows which sport 30 children liked playing best.

This can be represented as a pie chart.

Football	15
Hockey	8
Tennis	5
Running	2

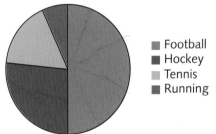

Favourite Sports

- Football
- Hockey
- Tennis
- Running

Football = $\frac{15}{30} \times 360 = 180°$

Tennis = $\frac{5}{30} \times 360 = 60°$

Running = $\frac{2}{30} \times 360 = 24°$

Quick Test

1. Look at the bar chart on page 76. How many more children like chicken flavour than ready salted flavour crisps?
2. Look at the line chart above. Which month had the least rainfall?

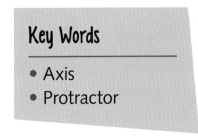

Key Words

- Axis
- Protractor

77

Timetables and Calculating the Mean

- Understand and interpret timetables
- Find the mean of a set of data

Interpreting Timetables

A timetable is a table showing the times for something such as buses, trains and school lessons. You can read a timetable to work out what you need to know, for example, what time the next bus arrives at the bus stop.

Example

The timetable below shows the route for the 131 Bus.

How long is the journey on Bus B from Langford Nook to Manor Junction?

	Bus A	Bus B	Bus C
Beech Avenue	8:05	9:30	11:00
Langford Nook	9:38	10:25	–
Cambridge Street	10:10	–	12:40
Manor Junction	11:42	11:40	13:15
Ardleven Square	12:35	13:15	14:30

If there is no time shown, then the bus does not stop at this bus stop.

Bus B leaves Langford Nook at 10:25. It arrives at Manor Junction at 11:40.

11:40 – 10:25 = The bus takes 1 hour 15 mins.

Using this timetable you can work out how long the bus takes between each stop and the length of the total journey.

Calculating the Mean

The **mean** of a set of data is the 'usual' or 'average' amount. The mean of a set of results can be found by adding up the results and dividing them by the number of results.

Key Point

The 'mean' is the average of a set of data.

Example

Patrick played in five football matches. Here is a record of the goals he scored:

Game 1	Game 2	Game 3	Game 4	Game 5
2 goals	3 goals	1 goal	3 goals	1 goal

Patrick scored 10 goals in total (2 + 3 + 1 + 3 + 1).

Calculate the mean number of goals per game by dividing the total number of goals (10) by the number of games played (5).

$$10 \div 5 = 2$$

The **mean** number of goals scored per game = 2

Patrick 'usually' scores two goals per game. So, on average he scores two goals per game.

Quick Test

Answer questions 1 and 2 using the timetable on page 78.

1. Which buses could you catch to get to a meeting in Manor Junction at 12:00?
2. How long does it take Bus A to get from Langford Nook to Ardleven Square?
3. Calculate the mean rainfall for a week:

Sun	Mon	Tue	Wed	Thu	Fri	Sat
5 mm	0 mm	6 mm	5 mm	8 mm	2 mm	2 mm

Key Word

• Mean

Practice Questions

To answer these questions you need to look at the graphs and charts on pages 76–77.

Challenge 1

1 How many children like ready salted flavour crisps best? _____20_____ ☐ 1 mark

2 Estimate how many children like cheese and onion flavour crisps best. _____88_____ ☐ 1 mark

3 How much rain fell in July? _____15_____ ☐ 1 mark

4 In which month was the highest rainfall recorded? _____December_____ ☐ 1 mark

5 What is the least favourite sport? _____running_____ ☐ 1 mark

6 What is the mean of these three numbers?

_____6_____ ☐ 1 mark

Challenge 2

1 Estimate how many more children like cheese and onion flavour than ready salted flavour crisps. _____68_____ ☐ 1 mark

2 Estimate how many children like salt and vinegar flavour crisps. _____65_____ ☐ 1 mark

3 How much more rain fell in August than April? _____9_____ ☐ 1 mark

4 What fraction of children prefer hockey? $\frac{8}{30}$ ☐ 1 mark

5 Find the mean of this set of data:

_____7_____ ☐ 1 mark

Challenge 3

1 During how many months was the rainfall over 15 mm? _____3_____ ☐ 1 mark

2 What fraction of children prefer tennis? $\frac{1}{6}$ $\frac{5}{30}$ ☐ 1 mark

3 What percentage of children prefer football? _____50%_____ ☐ 1 mark

4 Find the mean of this set of data:

4.5 6 5 6.5 4 4   32   _____5_____ ☐ 1 mark

5 The mean of a set of data is 8.

What is the fourth number? 10   8   6   ?   _____8_____ ☐ 1 mark

1   What are the coordinates of points P, Q, R and S?

P (__O__ , __12__) ✓

Q (__-14__ , __7__) ✓

R (__-6, 3__) ✗

S (__-8__ , __-3__) ✓

4 marks

2   ABCD are the vertices of a square Y.

What are the coordinates of point D?

D (__-5__ , __5__)

1 mark

3   a)   Translate shape Z 2 units left and 3 units up to produce shape Z'. What are the coordinates of the vertices of Z'?

(__-12__ , __8__)

(__-12__ , __-2__)

(__-7__ , __-2__)

3 marks

   b)   Reflect Z in the y axis to produce shape Z''. What are the coordinates of the vertices of Z''?

(__5__ , __-5__) (__10__ , __-5__) (__10__ , __5__)

3 marks

PS 4   Here are two identical squares. What are the coordinates of points L and M?

L (__5__ , __9__)

M (__2__ , __9__)

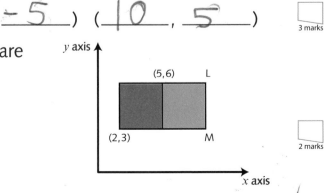

2 marks

81

Ratio and Proportion

- Understand ratios
- Simplify ratios
- Understand ratio tables

Understanding Ratio

A **ratio** is the quantitative relationship between two amounts.

'The ratio of boys to girls in the class is 1:2' means for every one boy there are two girls.

Example

Emily is threading beads onto a necklace. For every one red bead, she puts on two blue beads.

Ratio of red to blue beads = 1:2

She has five red beads and nine blue beads. Can she continue her necklace in the ratio of 1 red:2 blue?

No – she needs another blue bead. You can work out how many blue beads she needs to match five red beads.

To get from 1 to 5, you multiply the red side by 5 so you must do the same to the blue side: 2 × 5 = 10

Ratio of red to blue = 5:10

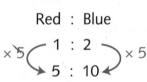

Red : Blue

×5 ⟨ 1 : 2 ⟩ × 5
  5 : 10

Simplifying Ratios

You can **simplify** ratios in the same way you simplify fractions.

Example

To simply 6:18 you need to look for something you can divide both sides by. This is where your multiplication and division facts come in handy!

÷6 ⟨ 6 : 18 ⟩ ÷6
  1 : 3

So 6:18 simplifies to 1:3

Key Point

When simplifying, always remember to do the same thing to both sides of your ratio.

You can **scale up** ratios too. This means you can work out how many of something there are from a given ratio.

Example 1

The ratio of boys to girls in a class of 32 children is 3 : 5.

$\times 4 \overset{3\ :\ 5}{\underset{12\ :\ 20}{}} \times 4$

So, there are 12 boys and 20 girls.

Example 2

Tanisha draws a triangle. The ratio of the sides is 3 : 4 : 8.

She then draws a triangle six times bigger. What are the lengths of the sides of the new triangle?

$\times 6 \overset{3\ :\ 4\ :\ 8}{\underset{18\ :\ 24\ :\ 48}{}} \times 6$

The side lengths of the new triangle are 18 : 24 : 48

Ratio Tables

You can use ratio tables to help set out your work logically.

Example

Jane made a smoothie with a ratio of 2 bananas : 3 apples. How many apples will she need if she uses 12 bananas?

By experimenting with the top row and doing the same to the bottom row, you can find out how many apples Jane would need.

She will need 18 apples.

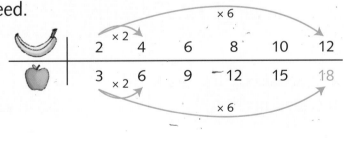

Quick Test

1. Oliver wants to thread beads in a ratio of red to blue of 3 : 5. He has nine red beads. How many blue beads does he need?
2. Simplify the ratio 24 : 6.
3. Looking at the ratio table above, how many bananas does Jane need to make a smoothie with 12 apples?

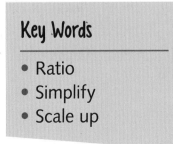

Practice Questions

PS **Problem-solving questions**

PS **1** How many red beads does Aisha need to make a necklace
in the ratio of 2:3 (black:red) if she has 12 black beads?

_____

1 mark

2 Simplify this ratio   6:24

_____

1 mark

PS **3** A recipe says you need flour and butter in the ratio
of 1:2. If you have 400 g of butter, how much flour
will you need?

_____

1 mark

4 3:9 is the same ratio as 1:____

1 mark

1 Does 15:25 fit the same ratio as 3:6? Give a reason for your answer.

_____

1 mark

PS **2** How many yellow beads does Aisha need to make a necklace
in the ratio of 2:4 (yellow:red) if she has 20 red beads?

_____

1 mark

3 Simplify this ratio   64:24

_____

1 mark

PS **4** A recipe says you need flour, butter and sugar
in the ratio of 3:2:1. If you have 600 g of butter,
how much flour and sugar will you need?

Flour: _____   Sugar: _____

2 marks

1 A ratio of 3:5:2 has been scaled up to 15:25:10.
What factor has it been scaled up by?

_____

1 mark

2 Simplify this ratio to its simplest form   42:14:7

_____

1 mark

PS **3** A recipe has the following ingredients.
It feeds four people.

How much of each ingredient do you
need if you want to make enough to
feed 10 people?

Ham	50 g	_____
Cream	100 ml	_____
Pasta	250 g	_____

3 marks

4 Which ratio is the same as 18:24:12? Tick the correct answer.

9:12:4 ☐   6:12:4 ☐   3:4:2 ☐

1 mark

1   Look at the graph.

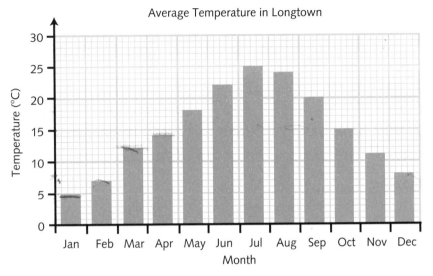

Average Temperature in Longtown

a) Which month has the lowest temperature? _____

b) How many months show a temperature of
    over 15°C? _____

c) How much warmer is it in July than December? _____

d) What is the mean temperature for the first
    three months of the year? _____

2   Look at the timetable.

	Kennedy Row	Gatsby Rise	Elm Road	Tibbs Avenue	Unicorn Close
Bus A	09:15	10:20	10:49	11:03	12:10
Bus B	10:35	11:10	–	11:59	13:25

a) How long does it take Bus A to get from
    Kennedy Row to Tibbs Avenue? _____

b) Which bus reaches Unicorn Close from
    Kennedy Row in the shortest time? _____

c) Why is there no time listed for Bus B at Elm Road?

_____

Solving Equations

- Find missing numbers and work out more complicated equations
- Work out a sequence of numbers
- Find pairs of numbers that satisfy an equation with two unknowns

Missing Numbers

In maths and science, unknown numbers are often replaced by symbols or letters. The symbol x is often used in algebra.

$x + 10 = 12$ ← x must equal 2.

Key Point

A curly x is used in algebra so that it doesn't get confused with a × (multiplication) sign.

Example

Look at this triangle. What is the value of x?

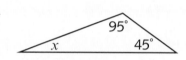

The interior angles of a triangle total 180°.

So you can write an **equation** to calculate the value of x:

$95° + 45° + x = 180°$

$140° + x = 180°$

$x = 180° - 140°$

$x = 40°$

$x = ?$

Number Sequences

Sometimes you can calculate a sequence of numbers by changing the value of the **variable**, n.

Example

If you change the value of n, you can calculate new values for $n + 5$.

n	1 2 3 4 5 6.....
$n + 5$	6 7 8 9 10 11.....

Working Out More Complicated Equations

Sometimes equations are more complicated and you need to rearrange them before you can work out the answer.

Example

$3a + 5 = 23$

To calculate the value of a, you need to reorganise your equation to keep symbols on one side and numbers on the other:

$3a = 23 - 5$ ← To move the 5 to the other side, you take away 5 from both sides:
$3a + 5 - 5 = 23 - 5$
$3a = 23 - 5$

$3a = 18$

$a = 6$

Equations with Two Unknowns

Sometimes you will come across a problem which has more than one solution.

Example

$a + b = 7$

The solution for this problem is all the number bonds for 7:

1, 6   2, 5   3, 4

$ab = 8$

The solution for this problem is all the factors of 8:
1, 8   2, 4

$a + b$

Quick Test

1. Find a:
   a) $5a + 1 = 16$ b) $3a - 2 = 10$ c) $6 + 2a = 20$

2. For the variables 1 to 5, calculate $2n + 3$.

Key Words

• Equation
• Variable

Practice Questions

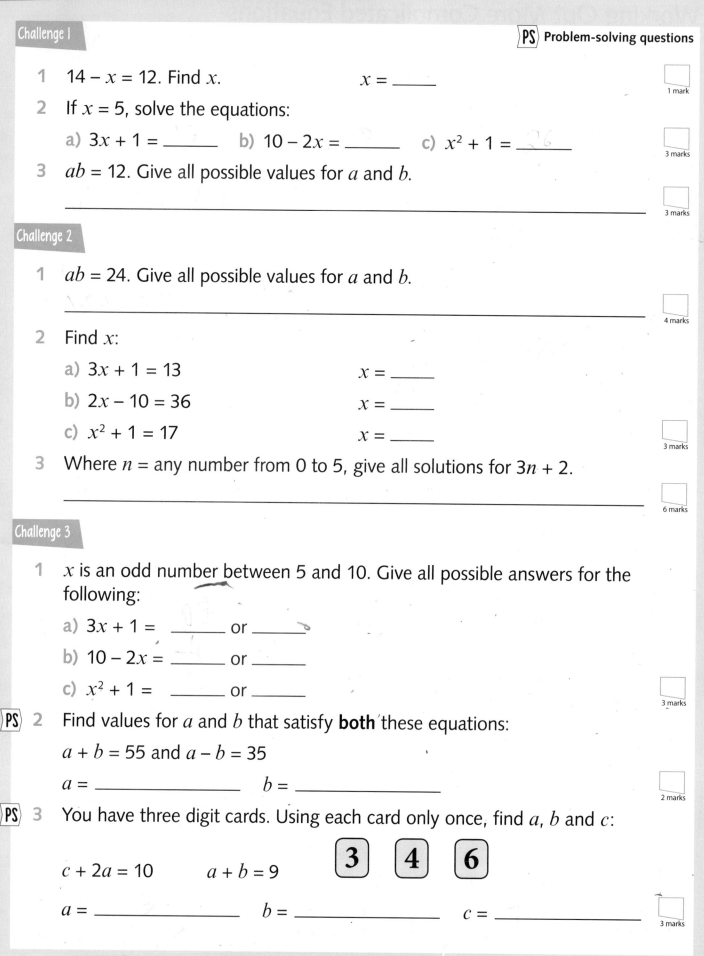

> PS Problem-solving questions

1 $14 - x = 12$. Find x. $x =$ _____ 1 mark

2 If $x = 5$, solve the equations:

  a) $3x + 1 =$ _____ b) $10 - 2x =$ _____ c) $x^2 + 1 =$ _____ 3 marks

3 $ab = 12$. Give all possible values for a and b.

  _____ 3 marks

Challenge 2

1 $ab = 24$. Give all possible values for a and b.

  _____ 4 marks

2 Find x:

  a) $3x + 1 = 13$ $x =$ _____

  b) $2x - 10 = 36$ $x =$ _____

  c) $x^2 + 1 = 17$ $x =$ _____ 3 marks

3 Where $n =$ any number from 0 to 5, give all solutions for $3n + 2$.

  _____ 6 marks

Challenge 3

1 x is an odd number between 5 and 10. Give all possible answers for the following:

  a) $3x + 1 =$ _____ or _____

  b) $10 - 2x =$ _____ or _____

  c) $x^2 + 1 =$ _____ or _____ 3 marks

PS **2** Find values for a and b that satisfy **both** these equations:

  $a + b = 55$ and $a - b = 35$

  $a =$ _____ $b =$ _____ 2 marks

PS **3** You have three digit cards. Using each card only once, find a, b and c:

  $c + 2a = 10$ $a + b = 9$ | 3 | | 4 | | 6 |

  $a =$ _____ $b =$ _____ $c =$ _____ 3 marks

Review Questions

1   Draw arrows between the columns to match these ratios.
    One has been done for you.

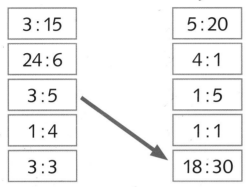

3 : 15	5 : 20
24 : 6	4 : 1
3 : 5	1 : 5
1 : 4	1 : 1
3 : 3	18 : 30

4 marks

2   Simplify these ratios:

    a) 24 : 3   _____

    b) 15 : 50   _____

    c) 8 : 36   _____

3 marks

PS 3   Amelia's recipe has the following ingredients:

    Cream   250 g
    Sugar   100 g
    Raspberries 75 g

    Amelia wants to make double the quantity. How much of each ingredient
    does she need?

    Cream   _____

    Sugar   _____

    Raspberries _____

3 marks

PS 4   In a class of 36 children, the ratio of boys to girls is 4 : 5.
        How many boys are in the class?

    _____

1 mark

5   Asif is making chocolate crispy cakes. He needs 100 g
    of crispies for each 50 g chocolate bar. If he uses 550 g
    of crispies, how much chocolate does he need?   _____

1 mark

Review Questions

PS Problem-solving questions

1 If $x = 5$ and $y = 3$, find $3x - 2y$.

______________ 1 mark

2 Fill in the missing number:

110 – ______________ = 50 + 30 1 mark

3 If a is an **odd number less than 10**, give all possible values for $3a - 1$.

______________ 5 marks

4 If $a = 3$ and $b = 8$, find $5a - b$.

______________ 1 mark

5 $ab = 30$. Find all possible values for a and b.

______________ 4 marks

6 Solve $3a - 3 = 24$

$a =$ ______________ 1 mark

PS 7 a and b are numbers greater than 3 but less than 10.

$a - b = b$

$2b = a$

Find values for a and b that solve both equations.

$a =$ ______________ $b =$ ______________ 2 marks

PS 8 $x + y + 2 = 10$

x and y are different **odd** numbers. Give all possible answers.

______________ 2 marks

9 Fill in the missing number:

35 + 20 = 67 – ______________ 1 mark

10 Solve $4a + 8 = 20$

$a =$ ______________ 1 mark

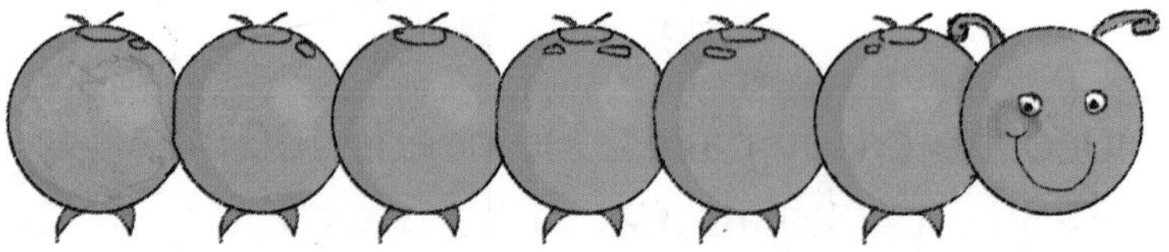

Mixed Questions

1 Order these decimals from the smallest to the largest:

3.13   3.01   31.0   3.113   3.0

_____   ☐ 1 mark

PS 2 Use each card **once** to make two-digit numbers that make these statements correct.

    3   6   5

3 ☐ > ☐ 4

58 < ☐ 2   ☐ 1 mark

PS 3 Petra buys **three** bananas. She gets 13p change from a pound. How much does **one** banana cost? _____ p   ☐ 1 mark

4 Put '+' or '−' signs in the spaces to make the statement correct:

14 _____ 6 _____ 3 _____ 5 = 22   ☐ 1 mark

PS 5 An orange costs 25p more than an apple. Chloe buys two apples and an orange for 85p. How much does an orange and an apple cost?

Apple: _____ p

Orange: _____ p   ☐ 2 marks

PS 6 Ike has 272 books to fit onto his book shelves. If 16 books fit on each shelf, how many shelves will he fill?

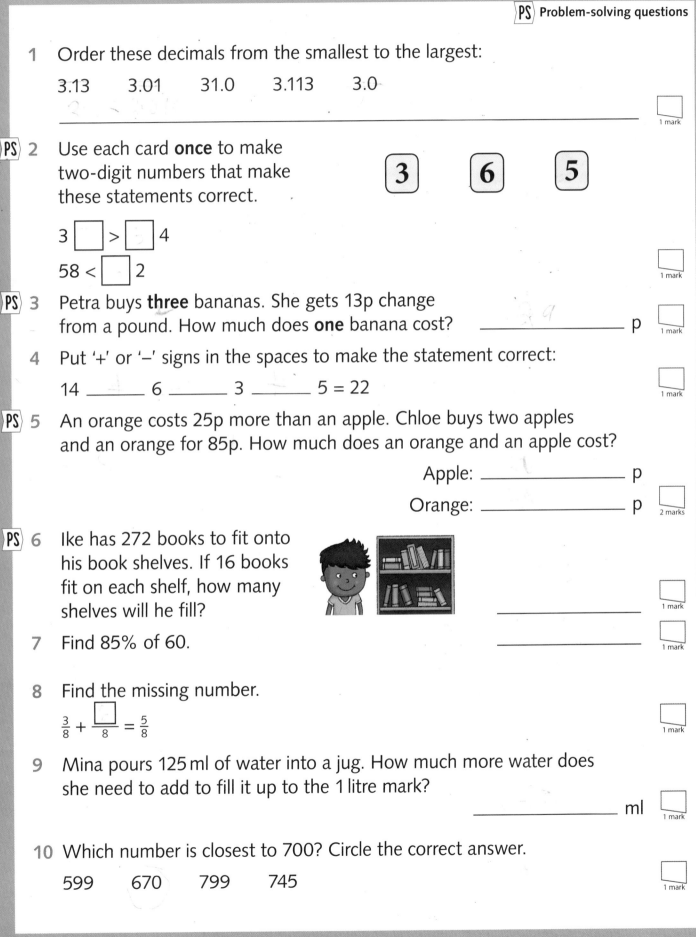

_____   ☐ 1 mark

7 Find 85% of 60.   _____   ☐ 1 mark

8 Find the missing number.

$\frac{3}{8} + \frac{\boxed{}}{8} = \frac{5}{8}$ ☐ 1 mark

9 Mina pours 125 ml of water into a jug. How much more water does she need to add to fill it up to the 1 litre mark?

_____ ml   ☐ 1 mark

10 Which number is closest to 700? Circle the correct answer.

599   670   799   745   ☐ 1 mark

Mixed Questions

11 Translate triangle A to A' moving 3 units left and 2 units down. Give the coordinates of the vertices of A'.

(_____ , _____)

(_____ , _____)

(_____ , _____) 3 marks

12 What temperatures do A and B point to on the scale?

↑A   −6°C   ↑B   0°C

A: _____

B: _____ 2 marks

PS 13

Oranges
35p each

Guenna buys six oranges and a smoothie.
She gets 34p change from £5.00.
How much did the smoothie cost?   £ _____ 1 mark

PS 14 Graham has £84.19 in his bank account. He spends £47.95 on new trainers. How much money does he have left?   £ _____ 1 mark

PS 15 Footballs cost £13.75 each. If Mr Flash, the PE teacher, wants to buy 15 new ones, how much will they cost? £ _____ 1 mark

PS 16 A school has 420 pupils and 30 teachers. It hires some 70-seater coaches to take everyone to a pantomime. How many coaches does it need to hire? _____ 1 mark

17 What is $\frac{3}{8}$ of 128?   _____ 1 mark

18 $\frac{3}{12} \times \frac{1}{4} = $ [ ] 1 mark

19 Mike travels to school on the 8.40 a.m. bus. The journey takes 35 minutes. What time does Mike arrive at school?   _____ a.m. 1 mark

Mixed Questions

20 Use these four digit cards to make the greatest **even** number **greater** than 6000:

4   **3**   **7**   **5**

_____ 1 mark

21 Which letter equals 300 thousand on the scale?

0   A   B C   D   1 million _____ 1 mark

PS 22 Maura and Wahid each buy a drink.
Wahid gets 28p change from a pound
and Maura gets £3.65 change from £5.

How much did the drinks cost altogether?   £ _____ 1 mark

23 Maths books cost £7.85.
A teacher buys 12 for her Year 6 class.

How much do the books cost altogether?   £ _____ 1 mark

24 Brian wants to lay a path around the edge of his garden.
He uses paving stones that are 45 cm long. How many
stones does he need to buy for an 18 m path?

_____ 1 mark

25 Find 65% of 120.   _____ 1 mark

26 Adele put her cake into the oven
at 3.45 p.m. It's ready at 5.20 p.m.
How long did it take to bake?   _____ 1 mark

27 Give your answer as a mixed number. $\frac{3}{10} + \frac{4}{5}$ = _____ 1 mark

28 Work out angle x:

36°

$x°$ 42°

_____ 1 mark

Mixed Questions

29 Round 54.372 to one decimal place. _____
1 mark

30 Calculate:

$3 + 4 \times 2 - 4 =$ _____
1 mark

PS 31 I buy **two** marker pens and a notebook.
The notebook costs £3.60.
I get £1.16 change from £10.

How much does **each** marker pen cost? £ _____
1 mark

PS 32 Mina thinks of a number.
She subtracts 2.5 then doubles her answer.
She adds 7 and then halves her answer.
The number she is left with is 15.

What was her starting number? _____
1 mark

PS 33 Song books cost £9.85. If a teacher buys 16 for the choir, how much do the books cost altogether?

£ _____
1 mark

PS 34 Plastic cups are sold in packs of 12.
Bill needs 154 cups.

How many packs must he buy? _____
1 mark

PS 35 This year, Al's season ticket for Pilchester Rovers has increased by 25%. It cost £210 last year.

Ticket

What is the new price? £ _____
1 mark

36 $\frac{3}{7} + \frac{2}{7} = \boxed{}$
1 mark

37 Work out angle x:

48° x° 24°

_____
1 mark

94

Mixed Questions

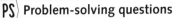

38 Fill in the missing numbers:

$55 \times 10 =$ _____

$1500 \div$ _____ $= 15$

_____ $\times 100 = 50\,000$

3 marks

39 What fraction does A point to on the scale?

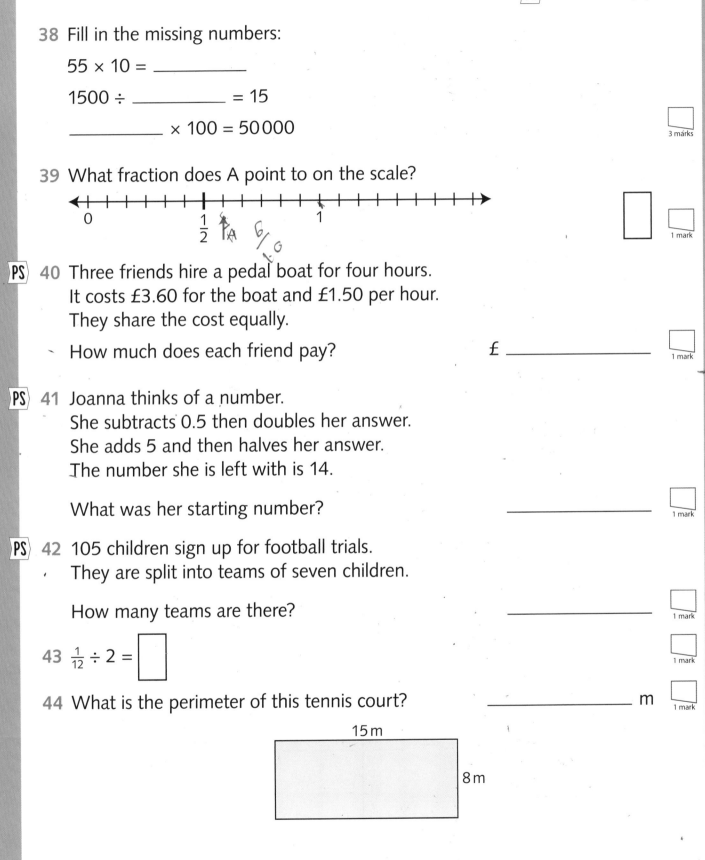

1 mark

PS **40** Three friends hire a pedal boat for four hours.
It costs £3.60 for the boat and £1.50 per hour.
They share the cost equally.

How much does each friend pay?

£ _____

1 mark

PS **41** Joanna thinks of a number.
She subtracts 0.5 then doubles her answer.
She adds 5 and then halves her answer.
The number she is left with is 14.

What was her starting number?

_____

1 mark

PS **42** 105 children sign up for football trials.
They are split into teams of seven children.

How many teams are there?

_____

1 mark

43 $\frac{1}{12} \div 2 = \boxed{}$

1 mark

44 What is the perimeter of this tennis court?

_____ m

1 mark

15 m

8 m

95

Mixed Questions

PS 45 What number does A point to on the scale? Estimate what number B points to.

−50   ↑A   ↑B   100

A: _____   B: _____

2 marks

46 Jina hires a bike for eight hours on holiday. How much does she pay?

£ _____

Bike Hire: £3.25 per hour.

1 mark

47 Fill in the blanks in this sequence.

6   13.5   _____   _____   36

2 marks

PS 48 Two rolls of ribbon are cut into lengths:

3 m roll of thin ribbon, 25 cm lengths

3 m roll of thick ribbon, 15 cm lengths

How many **more** pieces of the thick ribbon are there than thin ribbon?

_____

1 mark

PS 49 Zelda goes on a bike ride at 4.25 p.m. Her twin, Zainab, has to blow up her tyres and sets off 22 minutes later. If the trip takes 55 minutes, at what time do each of the girls reach their destination?

Zelda: _____

Zainab: _____

2 marks

50 Reflect shape B in the x axis to create shape B′.

What are the coordinates of the vertices of shape B′?

(_____ , _____)

(_____ , _____)

(_____ , _____)

(_____ , _____)

4 marks

Mixed Questions

51 Fill in the missing numbers.

$32 \times 10 =$ _____

$1300 \div$ _____ $= 130$

_____ $\times 100 = 3000$

3 marks

52 What decimals do A and B point to on the scale?

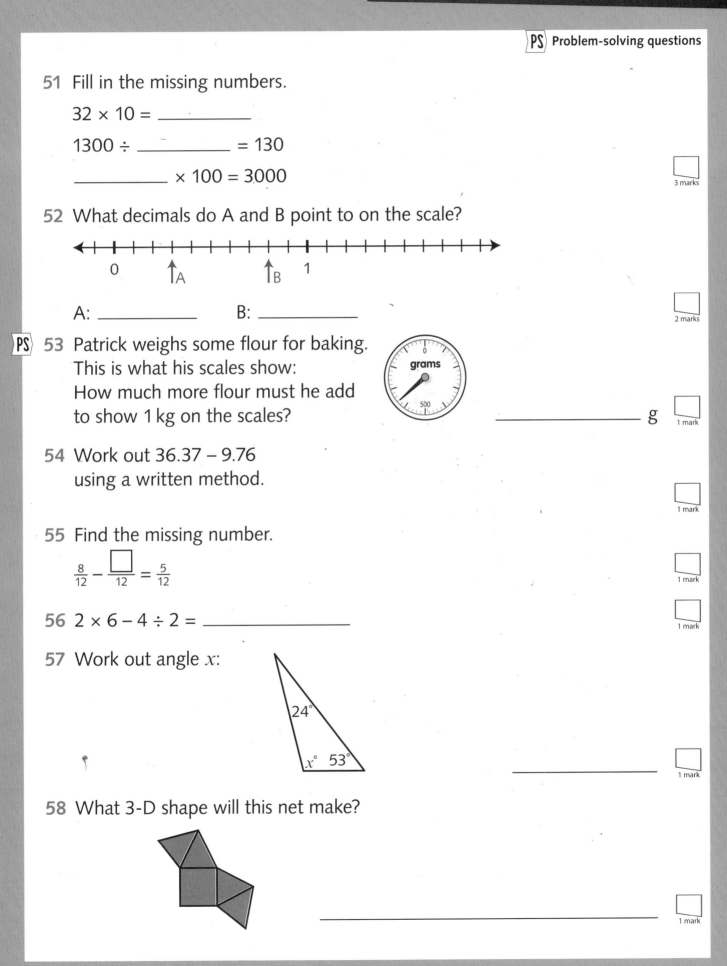

A: _____   B: _____

2 marks

PS **53** Patrick weighs some flour for baking. This is what his scales show: How much more flour must he add to show 1 kg on the scales?

grams

_____ g

1 mark

54 Work out $36.37 - 9.76$ using a written method.

1 mark

55 Find the missing number.

$\frac{8}{12} - \frac{\square}{12} = \frac{5}{12}$

1 mark

56 $2 \times 6 - 4 \div 2 =$ _____

1 mark

57 Work out angle x:

24°

$x°$ 53°

_____

1 mark

58 What 3-D shape will this net make?

_____

1 mark

59 Round 34.67 to the nearest whole number. _____ [ ] 1 mark

60 Which of the following are prime numbers?

  7   16   23   25   39   41 _____ [ ] 1 mark

PS 61 Benji wants to hire a bike for four hours. Which price plan is cheaper?

Price Plan A – Morning or afternoon £6.50, including helmet hire

Price Plan B – £1.25 per hour. Helmet hire £2.00

_____ [ ] 1 mark

62 Work out 48.35 – 8.48
using a written method. [ ] 1 mark

63 Change these mixed numbers to improper fractions:

  $1\frac{4}{5}$ [ ] $2\frac{3}{8}$ [ ] $1\frac{7}{10}$ [ ] $3\frac{4}{7}$ [ ] [ ] 4 marks

64 $\frac{3}{4} \times \frac{1}{3} =$ [ ] [ ] 1 mark

PS 65 What is the perimeter of the dinosaur paddock?

_____ m

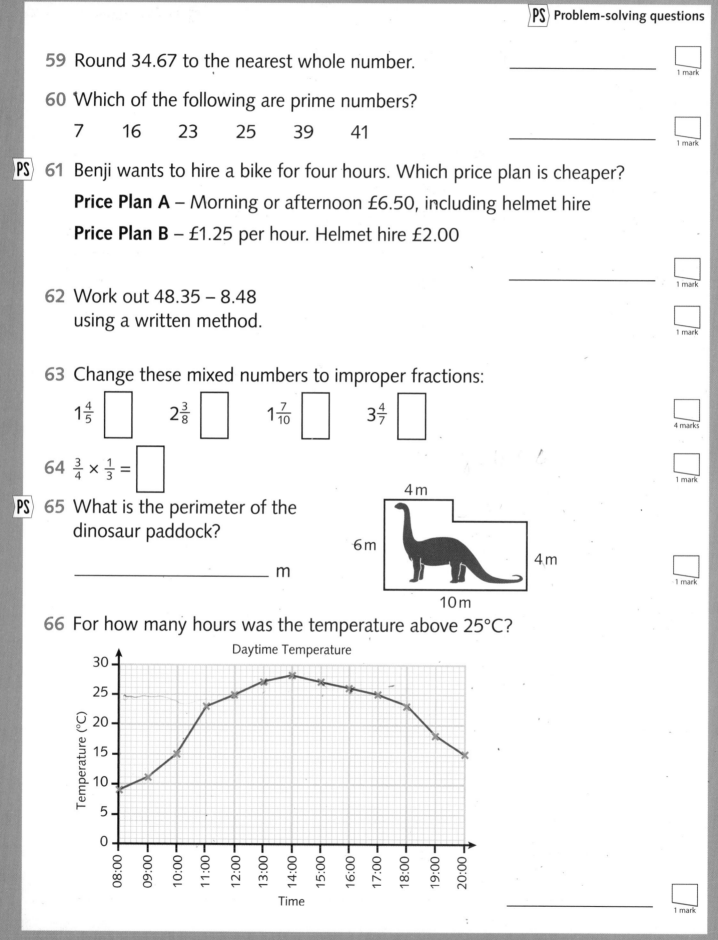

[ ] 1 mark

66 For how many hours was the temperature above 25°C?

Daytime Temperature

_____ [ ] 1 mark

Mixed Questions

67 Order these amounts from the smallest to the largest:

£2.30   32p   £3.20   £32   £2.33

_____

1 mark

68 Round 676 328 to the nearest 10 000.   _____

1 mark

PS **69** Yasmin buys a ruler and two highlighters.
She gets £1.64 change from £5. The ruler cost 98p.

How much did **one** highlighter cost?   _____

1 mark

PS **70** Skateboard equipment costs the following:

Helmet	£11.50
Gum shield	£3.75
Wrist guard (per pair)	£1.65
Shin pad (per pair)	£3.85

How much does Saran pay if he buys everything
on the list?   £ _____

1 mark

PS **71** A builder needs 3600 slates for a roof.   Load: 500 Slates

How many loads must he buy?

_____

1 mark

72 $\frac{3}{15} + \frac{2}{5} = \boxed{}$

1 mark

PS **73** Calculate the perimeter of
Farmer Trott's field:

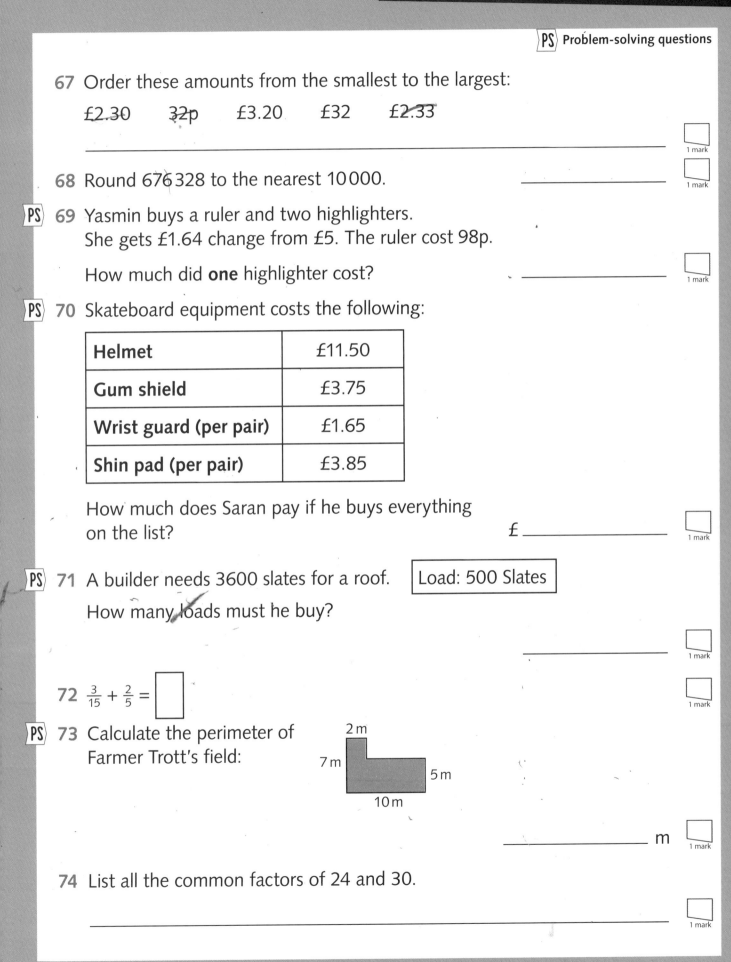

2 m

7 m

5 m

10 m

_____ m

1 mark

74 List all the common factors of 24 and 30.

_____

1 mark

75 Here are four cards: 2 7 6 8

Using **each** card once, make an **odd** number where the **thousands** value is less than 7. _____

1 mark

76 Which number is nearest to 20 000? 18 999 or 21 003. Give a reason for your answer.

_____

1 mark

PS 77 French dictionaries cost £15.75 each. Madame Mouchoir buys eight of them for her French club. How much does she spend altogether?   £ _____

1 mark

78 Work out 34.17 − 16.42 using a written method.

1 mark

PS 79 Fin buys some football boots marked at £55.00. The shop assistant tells him they are now 15% off. How much does Fin pay for his bargain boots?   £ _____

1 mark

80 $\frac{3}{4} + \frac{1}{6} = \boxed{}$

1 mark

PS 81 My buttons have a radius of 4 cm. My button snake is made up of nine buttons. How long is my button snake? _____

1 mark

82 This is from a recipe for four people. How much of each ingredient do I need if I want to make it for 10 people?

Pasta	100 g	_____ g
Sauce	80 g	_____ g
Cheese	120 g	_____ g

3 marks

83 Measure angle x.

_____

1 mark

Mixed Questions

84 What number does XXXVIII represent? _____ ☐ 1 mark

85 Put these fractions in order from smallest to largest:

$1\frac{1}{6}$ $\frac{3}{4}$ $\frac{7}{12}$ $\frac{4}{6}$

_____ ☐ 1 mark

86 Round 5682 to the nearest 1000. _____ ☐ 1 mark

PS 87 Peter is training for a 10 km run. This is his training log:

Week 1	Week 2	Week 3	Week 4
3.2 km	4.7 km	5.8 km	6.3 km

a) How many kilometres has he run after four weeks? _____ ☐ 1 mark

b) On average, how far did he run each week?

_____ km ☐ 1 mark

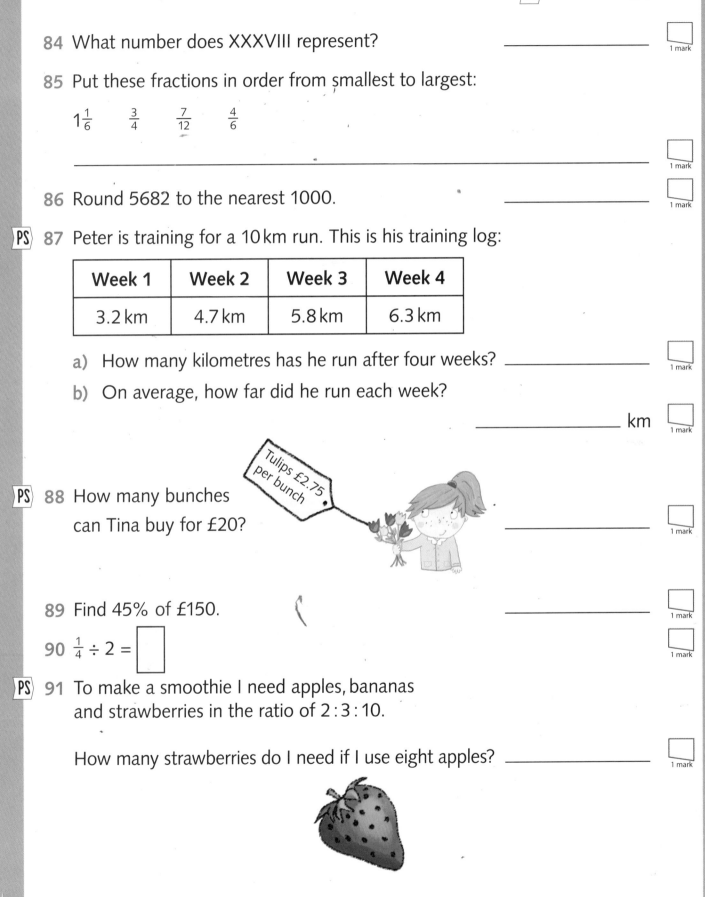

Tulips £2.75 per bunch

PS 88 How many bunches can Tina buy for £20? _____ ☐ 1 mark

89 Find 45% of £150. _____ ☐ 1 mark

90 $\frac{1}{4} \div 2 =$ ☐   ☐ 1 mark

PS 91 To make a smoothie I need apples, bananas and strawberries in the ratio of 2 : 3 : 10.

How many strawberries do I need if I use eight apples? _____ ☐ 1 mark

Answers

Quick Test page 5
1 a) 32946   b) 354693
2 a) ten   b) ten thousand   c) hundred
3 4335   4324   4315   4253   4135
4 a) 2315 < 4643   b) 5419 > 5416
   c) 32556 > 32546   d) 101322 > 10132

Quick Test page 7
1 −9 −5 −3 −2 0 5 6 10
2 4 1 −2 −5 −8 −11
3 −50 0 50 100 150

Quick Test page 9
1 a) 64320   b) 64300
   c) 64000   d) 100000

Quick Test page 10
1 a) 23   b) 46   c) 293
2 a) 1666   b) 1066   c) 1914

Practice Questions page 11

Challenge 1
1 46 228
2 107 170 701 710 1071
3 14, 9, 4, −1, −6, −11
4 a) 3430   b) 3400

Challenge 2
1 489
2 658, 685, 856, 865
3 1945

Challenge 3
1 17 $25\frac{1}{2}$ 34 $42\frac{1}{2}$ 51 $59\frac{1}{2}$
2 MDXXXVI
3 No, all units are either 2 or 7
4 a) 345640   b) 345600
   c) 350000   d) 300000

Quick Test page 13
1 a) 74   b) 22   c) 35
2 a) 79
   b) 38
   c) 447
   d) 266

Quick Test page 15
1 41
2 a) 168   b) 252   c) 243

Quick Test page 17
1 a) 407
   b) 1188
2 £47.05

Quick Test page 19
1 a) 651
   b) 674
   c) 3.87

Practice Questions page 20
Challenge 1
1 a) 55   b) 24   c) 83   d) 37
2 110
3 a) 8169
   b) 2152

Challenge 2
1 a) 535   b) 264
   c) 743   d) 334
2 262
3 a) 3908
   b) 39.88

Challenge 3
1 210
2 898
3 a) £61.66
   b) 5.38

Review Questions page 21
1 a) hundred   b) unit
   c) hundred
2 314 334 341 413 441
3 515 415 315 215
4 a) 60   b) 300   c) 1280
5 a) 400   b) 1200   c) 200
6 17 21.5 26 30.5 35 39.5
7 7 1 −5 −11 −17 −23
8 a) 50000   b) 20000   c) 150000
9 518 (18 greater, 478 is 22 less than 500)
10 No, all numbers in this sequence end in an
    even number
11 XXVII
12 a) 1936   b) 2018

Quick Test page 23
1 88 ÷ 11 = 8, 88 ÷ 8 = 11
2 1, 30, 2, 15, 3, 10, 5, 6
3 24
4 1, 2, 4

Quick Test page 25
1 9
2 64
3 2 and 7
4 23 or 29

Quick Test page 27
1 34 620
2 17.53
3 200

Quick Test page 29
1 660
2 1260
3 33 100
4 1887

Quick Test page 31
1 16
2 16.5
3 17

Practice Questions page 32
Challenge 1
1 1, 24, 2, 12, 3, 8, 4, 6
2 1, 2, 4, 8, 16
3 26 remainder 2
4 1245
5 36
6 37

Challenge 2
1 Any multiple of 15 (15, 30, 45, 60, 75, etc.)
2 192
3 $14\frac{6}{12}$ or $14\frac{1}{2}$
4 0.1365
5 8
6 1102

Challenge 3
1 2, 3 and 5
2 3744
3 125
4 15.5

Review Questions page 33
1 a) 74   b) 83   c) 48
2 663
3 667
4 a) 624   b) 255   c) 972
5 250
6 140
7 33
8 140
9 5639
10 £36.10
11 817
12 £19.37
13 £21.41

Quick Test page 35
1 a) $\frac{1}{3}$ b) $\frac{2}{3}$ c) $\frac{6}{5}$
2 $\frac{1}{6}$
3 $\frac{2}{12}$ $\frac{1}{4}$ $\frac{3}{6}$ $\frac{2}{3}$

Quick Test page 37
1 $\frac{10}{12} = \frac{5}{6}$
2 $\frac{1}{8}$
3 $\frac{11}{8}$
4 $\frac{1}{8}$

Quick Test page 39
1 0.35
2 3.6
3 8.4   8.43   8.55   8.57

Quick Test page 41
1 $\frac{9}{4}$
2 $1\frac{5}{7}$

Quick Test page 43
1 96
2 Science. (Science 60%, Maths 45%)
3 76%
4 25%

Practice Questions page 44
Challenge 1
1 8
2 2.6
3 $\frac{1}{4} = 0.25 = 25\%$

   $\frac{25}{75} = 0.33 = 33\%$

   $\frac{45}{90} = 0.5 = 50\%$
4 $\frac{7}{8}$
5 $1\frac{2}{5}$
6 0.56 0.6 0.61 0.65

Challenge 2
1 36
2 18.6
3 0.25 0.20 0.75
4 $\frac{7}{14}$ or $\frac{1}{2}$
5 $2\frac{1}{4}$

Answers

Challenge 3
1 40
2 52
3 $\frac{32}{35}$
4 $\frac{27}{8}$
5 $\frac{1}{4}$ $\frac{4}{12}$ $\frac{5}{6}$ $1\frac{1}{3}$

Review Questions page 45
1 80
2 2, 3, 5, 7, 11, 13, 17, 19
3 1904
4 2, 3 and 7
5 64
6 14.2
7 16
8 **a)** 35.47 **b)** 354.7 **c)** 3547
9 **a)** 165.9 **b)** 16.59 **c)** 1.659
10 1, 3, 5 and 15
11 91.2 cm

Quick Test page 47
1 350 mm
2 0.254 l
3 3450 grams
4 8 km

Quick Test page 49
1 30 cm
2 24 cm²

Quick Test page 51
1 36 cm²
2 90 cm³
3 56 743p

Quick Test page 53
1 19 : 35
2 180
3 28 July

Practice Questions page 54
Challenge 1
1 **a)** 250 mm **b)** 1.260 km
2 area = 24 cm²; perimeter = 20 cm
3 7.45 p.m.
4 £5.45

Challenge 2
1 **a)** 0.645 l **b)** 4126 g
2 area = 720 cm²; perimeter = 340 cm
3 40 cm
4 28 June

Challenge 3
1 2.5 m   3 23.5 km
2 48 cm³   4 17 cm²

Review Questions page 55
1 12   4 $\frac{8}{11}$
2 $\frac{3}{5}$
                        5 $\frac{1}{16}$
3 $\frac{16}{24}$
                        6 $\frac{1}{30}$
7 Jacob $\left(\frac{4}{5}\right)$
8 3.25 3.24 3.2 2.35 2.34
9 **a)** 23.7   **b)** 24
10 $2\frac{2}{5}$ 12 $\frac{75}{100}$ (or $\frac{3}{4}$); 0.75
11 $\frac{13}{4}$ 13 32

Quick Test page 57
1 540°
2 acute – a and c; obtuse – b, d and e
3 **a)** d   **b)** b

Quick Test page 59
1 $a = b = 78°$

Quick Test page 61
1
2 Cylinder

Quick Test page 63
1 B   2

Practice Questions page 64
Challenge 1
1 9 cm
2 30° (accept 28° to 32°)
3 60°
4 b

Challenge 2
1 Square-based pyramid
2 75° (accept 73° to 77°)
3 59°

Challenge 3
1 138° (accept 136° to 140°)
2 6.25 cm
3 Hexagonal-based prism

Review Questions page 65

1 cm or mm

2

mm	cm	m
35	3.5	0.035
270	27	0.27
3570	357	3.57

3 2.5 or 3 l

4 52 cm

5 42 cm

6 48 m²

7 a) £6.13
  b) 87p

8 5.45 p.m.

Quick Test page 67

1 x axis

2 (0,0)

3 A(2,5), B(5,6), C(4,1), D(1,3)

Quick Test page 69

1 Translation

2 A'(−5,5)

Quick Test page 71

1 Reflection

2 A'''(−5,−5),(−5,−10),(−15,−5)

Quick Test page 73

1 B(9,8), D(5,4)

2 E(2,5)

Practice Questions page 74
Challenge 1

1 A(2,4), B(4,5) and C(6,1)

2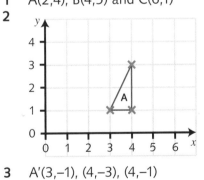

3 A'(3,−1), (4,−3), (4,−1)

4 (0,0)

Challenge 2

1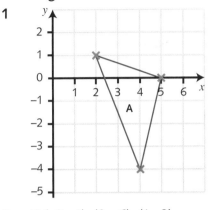

2 A' (−2,−1), (0,−6), (1,−2)

3 (2,2)

Challenge 3

1 Second quadrant

2 (4,4)

3 B(10,11), D(3,3)

Review Questions page 75

1 2 equal sides and 2 equal angles

2 35° (accept 33° to 37°)

3 a) cd and ef   b) none

4 25.6 cm

5 Tetrahedron (triangular-based pyramid)

6 $y = 100°$

7 b

Quick Test page 77

1 15

2 April

Quick Test page 79

1 Bus A or Bus B

2 2 hours 57 minutes

3 4 mm

Practice Questions page 80
Challenge 1

1 20

2 86–88

3 15 mm

4 December

5 Running

6 6

Challenge 2

1 66–68

2 64–66

3 9 mm

4 $\frac{8}{30}$ or $\frac{4}{15}$

5 7

2 $\frac{}{30}$ or $\frac{}{6}$

3 50%

4 5

5 8

Review Questions page 81

1 P(0,12), Q(–14,7), R(6,–3), S(–8,–8)

2 D(–5,5)

3 **a)** Z'(–12,–2), (–7,–2), (–12,8)
   b) Z''(5,–5), (10,–5), (10,5)

4 L(8,6), M(8,3)

Quick Test page 83

1 15

2 4:1

3 8

Practice Questions page 84
Challenge 1

1 18

2 1:4

3 200 g

4 1:3

Challenge 2

1 No 15:25 = 3:5 (3:6 = 15:30)

2 10

3 8:3

4 900 g flour, 300 g sugar

Challenge 3

1 5

2 6:2:1

3 Ham   125 g
   Cream   250 ml
   Pasta   625 g

4 3:4:2

Review Questions page 85

1 **a)** January
   b) 5 months
   c) 17°C
   d) 8°C

2 **a)** 1 hour 48 minutes
   b) Bus B
   c) It doesn't stop there

Quick Test page 87

1 **a)** $a = 3$ **b)** $a = 4$ **c)** $a = 7$

2 5, 7, 9, 11, 13

Practice Questions page 88
Challenge 1

1 $x = 2$

2 **a)** 16   **b)** 0   **c)** 26

3 1,12; 2,6; 3,4 or 12,1; 6,2; 4,3

Challenge 2

1 1,24; 2,12; 3,8; 4,6 or 24,1; 12,2; 8,3; 6,4

2 **a)** $x = 4$ **b)** $x = 23$ **c)** $x = 4$

3 2, 5, 8, 11, 14, 17

Challenge 3

1 $x = 7$ or 9;   **a)** 22,28   **b)** –4,–8   **c)** 50,82

2 $a = 45$ and $b = 10$

3 $a = 3$, $b = 6$ and $c = 4$

Review Questions page 89

1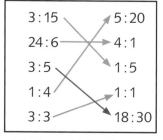

2 **a)** 8:1   **b)** 3:10   **c)** 2:9

3 Cream   500 g
   Sugar   200 g
   Raspberries   150 g

4 16 boys

5 275 g

Review Questions page 90

1 9

2 110 – 30 = 50 + 30

3 2, 8, 14, 20, 26

4 7

5 1,30; 2,15; 3,10; 5,6 or 30,1; 15,2; 10,3; 6,5

6 $a = 9$

7 $a = 8$ and $b = 4$

8 1,7 or 3,5

9 35 + 20 = 67 – 12

10 $a = 3$

Mixed Questions page 91

1 3.0   3.01   3.113   3.13   31.0

2 3$\underline{5}$ > 3$\underline{4}$, 58 < $\underline{6}$2

3 29p

4 14 + 6 – 3 + 5 = 22

5 Orange 45p; Apple 20p

6 17

7 51

8 $\frac{2}{8}$

9 875 ml

Answers

10 670

Mixed Questions page 92
11 (−16,4), (−6,4), (−16,9)
12 A: −9°C; B: −2°C
13 £2.56
14 £36.24
15 £206.25
16 6.43 = 7 coaches
17 48
18 $\frac{3}{48}$ or $\frac{1}{16}$
19 9.15 a.m.

Mixed Questions page 93
20 7534
21 B
22 £2.07
23 £94.20
24 40
25 78
26 1 hr 35 min
27 $1\frac{1}{10}$
28 102°

Mixed Questions page 94
29 54.4
30 7
31 £2.62
32 14
33 £157.60
34 13
35 £262.50
36 $\frac{5}{7}$
37 108°

Mixed Questions page 95
38 550
100
500
39 $\frac{7}{12}$
40 £3.20
41 12
42 15
43 $\frac{1}{24}$
44 46 m

Mixed Questions page 96
45 A: −20; B: in the range of 64 to 66
46 £26
47 21   28.5
48 8 more
49 Zelda: 5.20 p.m.;   Zainab: 5.42 p.m.
50 (8,−5), (13,−5), (8,−8), (13,−8)

Mixed Questions page 97
51 320   10   30
52 A: 0.3   B: 0.8
53 360 g
54 26.61
55 $\frac{3}{12}$

56 10
57 103°
58 Square-based pyramid

Mixed Questions page 98
59 35
60 7, 23, 41
61 Plan A is cheaper (B = £7)
62 39.87
63 $\frac{9}{5}$ $\frac{19}{8}$ $\frac{17}{10}$ $\frac{25}{7}$
64 $\frac{3}{12}$ or $\frac{1}{4}$
65 32 m
66 5 hours

Mixed Questions page 99
67 32p   £2.30   £2.33   £3.20   £32
68 680 000
69 £1.19 or 119p
70 £20.75
71 8
72 $\frac{9}{15}$ or $\frac{3}{5}$
73 34 m
74 1,   2,   3,   6

Mixed Questions page 100
75 2687, 2867, 6287 or 6827
76 18 999 is 1001 less than 20 000 (21 003 is 1003 more)
77 £126
78 17.75
79 £46.75
80 $\frac{11}{12}$
81 72 cm
82 Pasta   250 g
Sauce   200 g
Cheese   300 g
83 In the range 54° to 56°

Mixed Questions page 101
84 38
85 $\frac{7}{12}$, $\frac{4}{6}$, $\frac{3}{4}$, $1\frac{1}{6}$
86 6000
87 a) 20 km   b) 5 km
88 7
89 £67.50
90 $\frac{1}{8}$
91 40

Glossary

24-hour	Time recorded as 24 continuous hours, e.g. 1 p.m. = 13:00
3-D	A shape with three dimensions: length, width and height.

A

a.m.	Any time after 12 midnight until 12 noon or midday.
Acute	An angle measuring less than 90°.
Adjust	Make corrections to a calculation after rounding.
Analogue	12-hour time written as a.m. (morning) or p.m. (afternoon) usually shown by a clock with hands.
Angle on a straight line	Also called a straight angle. An angle on a straight line which = 180° e.g. ___⌒180°___
Anti-clockwise	The opposite direction to which the hands move around a clock
Area	The amount of material needed to cover a space. Units are usually cm², m², km², etc. and can be calculated in rectangles as $A = l \times w$
Axis	The horizontal (x axis) or vertical (y axis) lines used in plotting coordinates.

C

Capacity	The quantity that can be held in a container. Can also be known as volume and is recorded as units³ .
Carry	To move a digit to the next column in a calculation.
Circumference	The distance around a circle (perimeter).
Clockwise	The direction in which the hands move around a clock
Column method	Writing numbers in columns according to their place value to make them easier to add, subtract, etc.
Common factor	Numbers that are factors of more than one number (e.g. 5 is a common factor of 10 and 15).

Common multiple	Numbers that are multiples of more than one number (e.g. 12 is a multiple of 1, 2, 3, 4, 6 and 12).
Composite shape	A shape made from other shapes joined together.
Cube number	The result of multiplying a number by itself and by itself again, e.g. $4^3 = 4 \times 4 \times 4 = 64$

D

Decimal place	The number of digits to the right of a decimal point.
Decimal point	A 'full stop' that comes between the place values units and tenths.
Decompose	To split numbers into factors, e.g. decompose $6 = 2 \times 3$
Degrees	The units used to record angles, e.g. 90°.
Denominator	The number below the line in a fraction.
Diameter	The distance across a circle through the centre.
Digit	A number from 0 to 9.
Digital	Time expressed as digits, e.g. 9:15 instead of 'quarter past nine'.
Divisor	The number you are dividing by.

E

Equation	A number sentence where some numbers are replaced by letters, e.g. $2a = 6$
Equilateral	A triangle with three equal sides and three equal angles (all 60°).
Equivalent fraction	Fractions that equal each other, e.g. $\frac{2}{4} = \frac{1}{2}$
Estimate	A sensible guess at an answer.
Exchange	To change a number, e.g. change 40 into 30 and 10 to allow you to move it into another column to help in calculations.

F

Factor	Numbers that can be multiplied together to get another number (e.g. 2 and 3 are factors of 6).
Formula	Using letters or symbols where the letters can be replaced by

numbers, e.g. the formula for the area of a rectangle is $A = l \times w$

Fortnight Two weeks (14 days).

G

Greater than A larger value than another (>).

H

Hundreds The place value where that digit equals a number of hundreds.

I

Imperial A measurement system used before the decimal system (e.g. pints, ounces, etc.).

Improper fraction A fraction where the numerator is greater than the denominator, e.g. $\frac{7}{5}$
All improper fractions are therefore greater than one whole.

Irregular An irregular shape has sides of different lengths and interior angles that are not all equal.

Isosceles A triangle with two equal sides and two equal angles.

L

Latin alphabet The letters the Romans used to create their number system.

Leap year A year with an extra day on 29 February (366 days), which occurs every four years.

Least significant digit The digit with the lowest place value, e.g. 345.6**8**

Length A measure of the longest side of a shape measured in mm, cm, m, km, etc.

Less than A smaller value when compared against another (<).

Line of symmetry A line in which a shape can be reflected to give a mirror image of itself.

Lowest common denominator (LCD) The denominator that other denominators can be divided into or are multiples of.
The LCD of $\frac{1}{3}$, $\frac{1}{4}$ and $\frac{1}{6}$ is $\frac{1}{12}$ because all these fractions can be written with a denominator of 12
($\frac{1}{3} = \frac{4}{12}$, $\frac{1}{4} = \frac{3}{12}$ and $\frac{1}{6} = \frac{2}{12}$).

M

Mass How heavy something is, usually recorded in g or kg.

Mean The average or usual value of something calculated by totalling the values and dividing by the number of values, e.g. the mean of 2, 6 and 7 $= 2 + 6 + 7 = 15 \div 3 = 5$

Metric A measurement system based on decimals, e.g. 1 cm = 0.01 m, 1 kg = 1000 g, etc.

Midday The point in time between a.m. and p.m. recorded as 12 noon or 12:00 midday.

Midnight The point in time between p.m. and a.m. recorded as 12 midnight or 00:00

Mixed number A number containing a whole number and a fraction, e.g. $1\frac{1}{2}$

Most significant digit The digit with the greatest place value, e.g. **3**45.62

Multiple The result of multiplying a given number by any other number, e.g. multiples of 4 are 4, 8, 12, 16 … (the 4 times table answers).

Multiple of 10 A result of multiplying any whole number by 10, e.g. 10, 20, 30, 40 …

N

Negative number A number to the left of zero on a number line. Recorded with a minus (–) sign before it. (As the digits increase the number has less value, e.g. –10 is smaller than –5).

Net A 2-D representation of a 3-D shape opened up and folded out.

Number bonds The corresponding numbers needed to make a given total, e.g. number bonds to 10: 1,9; 2,8; 3,7; 4,6; 5,5.

Numerator The number above the line in a fraction.

O

Obtuse An angle greater than 90° but less than 180°.

Glossary

Origin — The point where the x and y axes meet with the coordinates (0,0).

P

p.m. — Any time after 12 noon or midday until 12 midnight.

Parallel — Lines which run the same distance apart and never meet.

Parallelogram — A four-sided shape (quadrilateral) where the opposite sides are parallel.

Partition — To split a number into its individual parts depending on their place value, e.g. 324 = 300 (3 hundreds), 20 (2 tens) and 4 units.

Percent — A value expressed as something 'out of' 100, e.g. 25% = 25 out of $100 = \frac{25}{100}$

Perimeter — The distance around the outside of a 2-D shape.

Perpendicular — A line lying at 90° to another line is said to be perpendicular to that line, e.g. Line A is perpendicular to Line B.

Line A

Line B

Place holder — A zero used to keep all digits in the correct column during multiplication.

Place value — The value each digit has, shown by its position.

Polygon — A shape with at least three straight sides.

Positive number — A number to the right of zero on a number line (e.g. 1, 2, 3, 4, etc.).

Prime factor — A factor which is also a prime number (e.g. 2 and 7 are prime factors of 14).

Prime number — A number which only has two factors, itself and 1, e.g. 2, 3, 5, etc.

Product — The result of multiplying two or more numbers, e.g. the product of 2, 4 and 3 is 24.

Properties — The features that describe a shape, e.g. the number and size of sides and angles.

Protractor — A device used to measure angles in degrees (°).

Q

Quadrant — One of four areas on a coordinate grid. Point (3,4) will be in the first quadrant; (3,−4) will be in the fourth quadrant.

Quadrilateral — A four-sided shape.

R

Radius — The distance from the edge of a circle to its centre.

Ratio — The relationship between two amounts, e.g. the ratio of boys : girls is 3 : 2.

Reflection — The mirror image of a shape after it has been reflected in a line.

Reflex — An angle greater than 180° but less than 360°.

Regular — A regular shape has sides all the same length and all internal angles are equal.

Remainder — The amount left over after a division calculation, e.g $10 \div 3$ = 3 remainder 1

Rhombus — A four-sided shape where opposite sides are parallel and all sides are of equal length.

Right angle — An angle equalling 90°.

Rounding — Adjusting a number to the nearest 10, 100, etc. to make it easier to calculate with.

Round down — Reducing a number to the nearest 10 or 100 below it, e.g. 34 would round down to 30.

Round up — Increasing a number to the nearest 10 or 100 above it, e.g. 36 would round up to 40.

S

Scalene — A triangle where none of its sides or angles are equal.

Scale up — Multiplying by a set number to increase quantities, e.g. scale up the ratio 3 : 2 by 2 = 6 : 4

Sequence	A set of numbers that increase or decrease by the same value each time.
Simplify	To reduce a fraction to its simplest form by dividing the numerator and denominator by the same amount, e.g. $\frac{8}{24} = \frac{1}{3}$
Square number	The result of multiplying a number by itself, e.g. $3^2 = 3 \times 3 = 9$
Symbol	A shape or letter that represents a number.
Symmetrical	A shape where one side is the mirror image of the other.

T

Tens	The place value where that digit represents a number of tens.
Term	The corresponding number in a sequence, e.g. the third term of the sequence 1, 3, 5, 7 is 5.
Translation	To move a shape's position or direction without altering its original size or its shape.
Trapezium	A four-sided shape where one pair of opposite sides is parallel.

U

Units	The 'ones' place value. The system used to record measurements, e.g. the units for time are hours, minutes and seconds. The units for length are mm, cm and m.

Units³	The units of measurement for a cubed number.

V

Variable	A number that can change depending on what value it is given.
Vertex (vertices)	The corner(s) of a 2-D or 3-D shape.
Vertically opposite	The angles opposite each other when two lines cross. They are equal.
Volume	The quantity that can be held in a container and recorded as units³ (calculated by $l \times w \times h$ in a cuboid).

W

Whole number	A number that does not have any fraction or decimal parts, e.g. 34, 5, 126.

X

***x* axis**	The horizontal axis used when plotting coordinates.

Y

***y* axis**	The vertical axis used when plotting coordinates.

Grid Paper for Page 74, Challenge 1 and 2

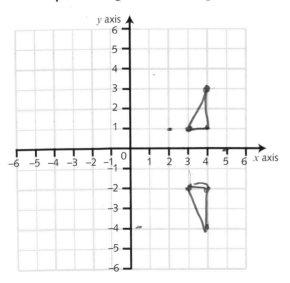

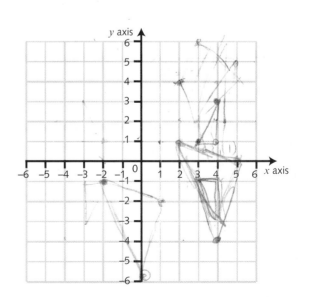

111

Index